How Are You Programmed?

How
Are You
Programmed?

J. EDWARD BARRETT

JOHN KNOX PRESS
Richmond, Virginia

Scripture quotations are from the *Revised Standard Version of the Bible,* copyrighted 1946 and 1952.

International Standard Book Number: 0-8042-0604-X
Library of Congress Catalog Card Number: 70-155782
© John Knox Press 1971
Printed in the United States of America

This book is dedicated
to my wife, *Suzanne,*
whose steadfast encouragement,
and to my daughters
Jeanne Heather (age 7),
whose charming consideration,
and *Betsy Sue* (age 4),
whose delightful interruptions,
all played their part in the writing of these pages.

Preface

This is a book about man. Like most such books, it was written as much to help the author understand himself as to help instruct others. Behind its writing is the confidence that a theological interpretation of man is a legitimate human enterprise, but that such legitimacy only follows after having considered seriously the information about man provided by the natural and social sciences.

This book, therefore, is the offspring of two important groups of thinkers. I gratefully acknowledge indebtedness to the fertile insights of scientific naturalism—particularly the interpretations of man outlined by Desmond Morris in *The Naked Ape,* by Konrad Lorenz in *On Aggression,* by Robert Ardrey in *African Genesis,* by Arthur Koestler in *The Ghost in the Machine,* and by Viktor Frankl in *Man's Search for Meaning.* For seminal ideas involving the theological interpretation of man I am indebted to Reinhold Niebuhr's *The Nature and Destiny of Man* and *The Self and the Dramas of History,* to Martin Buber's *I and Thou,* to John Cobb's *The Structure of Christian Existence,* to Pierre Teilhard de Chardin's *The Phenomenon of Man,* to Charles Hartshorne's *Reality as Social Process,* to Henry Nelson Wieman's *Man's Ultimate Commitment,* and to Paul Tillich's *The Courage to Be* and *Systematic*

Theology. My own thought does not simply repeat the conclusions of any of these men—but it is difficult for me to imagine my own thought without them. I have regularly taken the liberty to write in bold generalities. Typologies, developed for the sake of clarity, always allow for exceptions—of which the scholarly reader will be aware.

Portions of Chapter I were originally drafted as a paper read at a meeting of the Ohio Academy of Religion in 1969. The original draft of Chapter III was read at a divisional meeting of the American Academy of Religion in 1970. Similarly, the original draft of Chapter IV, now completely rewritten, was read at a divisional meeting of the American Academy of Religion in 1968. It was subsequently published under the title "A Theology of the Meaning of Life" by *Zygon: Journal of Religion and Science,* the University of Chicago Press, in June 1968.

Both the substance and the style of these chapters were forged in dialogue with my colleagues Russell S. Hutchison, William L. McClelland, Frank D. Minton, and Wilbur B. Franklin. For their critical astuteness and scholarly support I offer my unqualified thanks.

Contents

III. HOPE 70

IV. MEANING 96

How Are You Programmed?

I

PERSONAL FREEDOM

What does it means to be a man? The answer is not at all obvious. For biological evolution has produced man without publishing an operator's manual telling him what to do with himself. It is difficult to know how to interpret this oversight on evolution's part. Some animals appear to contain in the hieroglyphics of their genes rather definite instructions as to what it means to be, say, an amoeba, an ant, or an alligator. Other animals, such as dogs and apes, appear to have a somewhat incomplete set of instructions —so that they must fill in occasional blank pages with their own learning experience. The human animal is not *all* blank pages. But the fragments of instinctual instruction are so minimal, and the arrangement of those rare paragraphs so scattered, that man is unable to discern a general pattern of genetically programmed meaning, and is a mystery to himself.

Yet man wants to know. And so, from very ancient times, he has attempted to fill in the blank pages and to tie together his fragments of genetic programming with interpretive myths, legends, and cosmologies. Eventually these interpretive efforts reached a stage of sophistication wherein they became metaphysical systems, in which thinking was disciplined, sustained, and architectonic, suggesting a general pattern of meaning after all. Such metaphysical speculation attempted to go literally "beyond the physical" in order to discover a frame of meaning which would make sense of both the physical and that mysterious spectrum of subjective feelings sometimes vaguely described as "spiritual." But man's speculations beyond the physical sometimes seduced him into forgetting the physical. He became enchanted with writing idealistic metaphysical systems and occasionally found their composition easier, their logic tidier, and their attractiveness enhanced when the fragmentary instinctual paragraphs were omitted altogether.

Of Monkeys and Men

Then, in the nineteenth century, man rediscovered his neglected kinship with the animal world. Darwin established the human race's common origins with the primates. The metaphysical systems man had constructed seemed a rather pretentious undertaking for an animal who was, after all, only a monkey. Humbled by his heritage and embarrassed by his oversight, man resolved to abandon metaphysics. Only slowly—after a century of existential agonizing over "meaninglessness"—has it dawned upon him that what looked like it rendered an explanation to the meaning of manhood impossible was in fact its solution: *Man is the monkey who does metaphysics.* He has not always done them well. Perhaps he has never done them very well. He may be more than this. Perhaps he is much more than this. But no answer to the question as to what it means to be a man can henceforth ignore the fact that he is the animal who asks about the meaning of his manhood, and who speculates concerning the answer.

Of Spiders and Dogs

The fact that man is born without genetically programmed instructions determining the meaning of his life is of decisive importance for understanding what it means to be a man. In a way that is not true of any other animal, man is free. He is, in fact, the animal whom evolution has genetically programmed to be free from control by genetic programming. The considerably different ways in which men interpret their humanity—animist and atheist, oriental mystic and legalistic Jew, otherworldly pietist and secular Christian—evidence their freedom from a genetically assigned self-understanding.

This freedom of man is much more than a freedom to be confused. But freedom is confusing. Part of the confusion arises from the very nature of freedom itself. Those events or entities which are least confusing are those which are least free. They can be defined with precision because they are subject to control, measurement, prediction. Calculating the speed of falling objects, or the distance between two points, would provide obvious instances in which clarity can be at a maximum and confusion at a minimum. But the behavior of an individual human being in a cafeteria line is considerably less subject to calculation. Where freedom is least at issue precision of definition is optimal; where freedom is present ambiguity as well as possibility increases.

But there is a further and more serious difficulty in defining the meaning of freedom. For more than a century Western thought has been enamored with political freedom while being intimidated by philosophical determinism. "Determinism" is a calculating, mechanistic, reductionist world view. It likens men to lower animals, and lower animals to machines, judging all behavior to be reducible to causes, which are themselves determined by previous causes, which are themselves determined by . . . *ad infinitum.* Determinism claims "scientific" credentials for its view of the world. That claim must be challenged. More important, however, is the claim that freedom can be understood within the presuppositions of determinism. Freedom, so it is said, is not an alternative to determinism, but a noteworthy instance of it. The argument proceeds like this.

If we should see a spider in our garden, doing the things that spiders do, undeterred by externally imposed limitations, we should then be inclined to describe that spider as "free." Alternatively, we would *not* describe the spider as free if it were caught and placed in a glass jar or a small cage. In such instances, "freedom" means "without external constraint," and the lack of freedom is identical with the imposition of external constraint. In neither case, however, is determinism called into question. We take it for granted that the spider's behavior is genetically programmed, and that it is therefore determined behavior. The freedom of the spider is its freedom to be a spider doing those things that spiders do. But, of course, those things that spiders do are determined. Freedom is this noteworthy kind of determinism—self-determinism, unhindered by external constraints.

The same analysis, so it is said, applies to the freedom of men. Freedom is the freedom to be what we are, uncurbed by external threats or pressures. It is not opposed to determinism but is instead a noteworthy instance of it. Lee Harvey Oswald, for example, was free not to murder President Kennedy, since (so far as we know) no external force coerced him into doing so against his will. But since Oswald was Oswald, and not Pope John XXIII, it was determined by the constitution of his character that he should murder President Kennedy. He was free to do what he willed, but what he willed was determined by the makeup of his character. The freedom of Oswald was his freedom to behave the way his character determined he would behave. Freedom is thus defined as an instance of self-determinism, but determinism nevertheless.

Of course, the character and behavior of "higher" animals is far more complicated than the character and behavior of the spider, and the arguments of determinism take some of that complexity into account. The spider's behavior is determined by his genetic programming. The dog's behavior is not—at least not totally. The dog may be born with some genetically predisposed patterns of behavior, but he is also born with "open programming," intelligence, or the capacity to learn. His social experiences and history will program him in a way which may reinforce, may contradict, subvert, rechannel, or otherwise override his genetic programming. And therein lies the possibility of an extended meaning to "freedom."

If a dog has been trained to refuse food from strangers—in conflict with his natural appetite—he may or may not be comfortable with this condition. To the extent that he is not comfortable with it, he may, according to determinism, legitimately be described as not free. By this extended definition, *"freedom" means both freedom from external constraint and freedom from internal compulsions which distress the rest of the psychic organism.* A human example would appear in the kleptomaniac who does not intend to steal, but who nevertheless steals, and is distressed by his own actions. But it is not necessary to appeal to criminal illustrations. In the seventh chapter of Romans St. Paul describes the experience in words we can all appropriate: "I do not understand my own actions. For I do not do what I want, but I do the very thing I hate. . . . I can will what is right, but I cannot do it." When a man's total programming is short-circuited, or when some aspects of his programming put him at odds with other aspects of his programming, so that his actions express the triumph of compulsions rather than a response of the whole organism, we may rule him a victim of his internal circumstances and may declare him "not free." For to be free must mean freedom from internal compulsions which put me at odds with myself, just as it means freedom from external constraint which puts me at odds with my environment. But again, such freedom presupposes complete determinism. To say that a man is free is not to say that his behavior is uncaused; it is to declare him free to be himself, uncoerced from outside, unconstrained by destructive conflicts within.

This is the life proposed for freedom by the world view of determinism. The argument is full of clarity and capable of illuminating experience. There can be no doubt that much of human life *is* lived on levels of genetic and socio-historic programming. What I now wish to argue is that the analysis does not exhaust the meaning of "freedom," and that it totally fails to account for the decisively human kind of freedom—personal freedom—which distinguishes man from both the spider and the dog.

The Presiding Self and Symbols

By "personal freedom" I intend to designate an activity, probably limited on this planet to human existence, in which personal agents effectively preside over both their genetic and historic programming, and in so doing reprogram themselves and reorganize their world. This freedom of the human self to preside over its own activities certainly has "causes" in that it arises out of the biochemical organism and its history. But it *is* free from cause (or so I will argue) in that, while its biochemistry and history make it possible, its biochemistry and history do not determine how it will actualize itself. The presiding self has an undetermined (though limited) freedom within and over its biochemical and historical ground. In man we find evolution become conscious of itself, and determinism become free from itself. Another way to say this is that the evolutionary process has, in man, determined the *existence* of an organism whose *behavior* is undetermined.

Of course, to a considerable extent the behavior of man *is* determined by his genetic and historic programming. He shares much of his life with the rest of the animal kingdom. But the purpose of this chapter is to explore and emphasize that quality of life and level of existence which is unique to man and which is not finally determined by biochemistry or learning experience. Man is the animal capable of self-programming; he therefore transcends the biochemical and historic programming of the dog just as the dog transcends the merely genetic programming of the spider.

This means a critical challenging of the interpretation of freedom suggested by the illustration concerning Lee Harvey Oswald and President Kennedy. It is no doubt true (by definition) that the biochemistry and history of Oswald constituted his character and disposition. It *may* be true that Oswald was a victim of his nature and nurture, having no other choice than to obey his compulsions. But if this was the case, then the illustration is ill-conceived, defining the nature of man by appealing to an instance of insanity. Whether or not Oswald's biochemistry and history constituted the ground of a presiding self, capable of taking charge of his character and accountable for his actions, is a moot point—a matter of history which can hardly be decided now. But the presence of a presiding self in the lives of normal, healthy men is not settled by the appeal to its absence or ineffectiveness in Oswald. The power of a presiding self to exercise freedom over its own genetically and historically formed character no doubt varies from man to man—just as the strength of men's biceps vary. But the reality of this presiding self is what makes man man, and the exercise of its freedom is identical with the dignity of human existence.

How does this freedom of the human self actually come about? There is every reason to believe that even the lowest forms of animal life experience a rudimentary kind of selfhood, subjective awareness, or inner feelings—in a primitive way analogous to our own. Such an acknowledgment does not attribuite "thinking" to subhuman species. It simply takes seriously the continuity of evolution. The subjectivity of the spider is probably confined to an inner experience of the genetically programmed organism interacting with its environment. Such "feeling" serves to sensitize the spider to its environmentally triggered and genetically determined task.

The subjectivity of the dog must be a far more complex and developed experience. At least, it is reasonable to assume that the dog's inner feelings are much richer than the spider's because of the dog's additional capacity for historic programming. Nevertheless, in continuity with the spider, the subjective feeling of the dog must largely (if not totally) function to sensitize the whole organism to a task which is genetically and historically programmed, and triggered by its environment.

The character of subjectivity apparently increases in richness with progress up the evolutionary ladder, particularly accompanying increases in complexity of the nervous system. What I now want to suggest is that in man subjectivity reaches a degree of intensity such that it no longer functions simply to sensitize the organism to tasks which are genetically or historically determined, but is able to sensitize the organism to tasks which are largely mental—tasks which are subjectivity's own. Just as fetal cells divide and produce cells which differ, so man's subjectivity divides into functionally different forms of consciousness. In man subjectivity develops its own equivalent to "organs," and in addition to feeling and memory (present on lower levels), it develops symbol systems, reasoning, imagination, and above all (almost literally) the capacity to preside over these activities in such a way as (within limits) to override learning just as learning is able (within limits) to override instincts. But it is necessary to emphasize the parenthetical words "within limits." Against a deterministic behaviorism it is important to affirm the effective freedom of the human self to preside; while against those who believe in the unconditional freedom of a supernatural soul it is important to affirm that the self is biochemically grounded and functionally unstable, even undependable. In its strength the self is significant enough to distinguish the human animal. In its weakness it is simply absorbed into the level of the lower animal consciousness.

Personal freedom is a distinctive kind of freedom accompanying the evolution of a presiding self. It is directly dependent upon the presiding self's capacity to use symbols and concepts, words or their equivalent. Men are acutely uncomfortable with new experiences until these are named. This is because, ordinarily, verbal symbols both connect a man with his world and protect him from its charm and power. Insofar as such symbols designate events or entities in the world, they relate man to his world. But insofar as such symbols may be reflected upon and reorganized in isolation from and defiance of the events they designate, they insulate man from having to respond as programmed organism to environmental stimuli. For example, a man is able to designate and consider at length the ecology of polar bears while himself in a tropical rain forest. Because of words his entire attention—reading, reflecting, writing—may be absorbed with bears, snow, and ice. His actual environment may surround him with mosquitoes, heat, and tropical rain. He knows this, but has chosen to ignore it. Moreover, should the mosquitoes, heat, and rain become so oppressive that they do demand his attention, he is able to take the pattern of symbols which designates his world as experienced, rearrange them into an alternative pattern of possibility, and in pursuit of that new pattern enter a well-screened, air-conditioned hotel. It is because of verbal symbols that the presiding self is free. They both relate us to and insulate us from the charm and coercive power of the real world.

The spider and the dog have more immediate access to the experienced world. But the price they pay for this immediate access is to have their lives determined by the content of that experience. The spider's relationship to the world is not mediated by verbal symbols. But the other side of the spider's direct access to the world is the world's direct access to the spider. The circuit is closed and the relationship is mutually determined. And so the spider does what spiders—given such a world—have always done.

This need not mean that the spider's actions are totally determined or that novelty is absent. It may very well be that all of reality—from subatomic particles to human beings—enjoys some degree of "uncertainty" (Heisenberg), some latitude of openness that is undetermined within determined limits. In this sense, unpredictability may always be present—to the eternal frustration of those interested in mathematical precision and logical tidiness. Indeed, unless the universe below us is in this sense "open" we probably would have no room to creatively change it from above. But such openness, while providing for chance and novelty, is not itself personal freedom. Personal freedom is a particular kind of activity within that openness. It is the activity of a presiding self which is conspiring to transform the real world and which is protected from its charm and power by abstract symbols.

Because of these symbols, man is freed from having to respond as programmed organism to its experienced environment. Instead of relating directly to the outside world with its charm and power, man relates primarily to a "cool" world of concepts which is subject to his control. It is a disarmed but representative world of symbolic ambassadors through which man negotiates his uniquely free relationship to the real world. Verbal symbols both insulate man from being victimized by his world and permit him to make the world his victim. It is in fact no small point that what the P editor of Genesis portrays as man's "dominion" over the earth (Gen. 1:26) is paralleled by the J editor with a story in which Adam "names" every creature (Gen. 2:19). For verbal symbols are the weapons which permit us to disarm our world and achieve dominion over it. Because of them we are free.

Of course, symbols are not automatically free from the power of the entities or events they symbolize. Sometimes—as every demagogue knows—symbols have inordinate power, totally out of proportion to the reality they designate. Then the symbol leads to the domination of man rather than domination by him. The presiding self is capable of abstracting its symbols from the power of the symbolized to a point where they are functionally antiseptic. It does not always take the care to do this. To the extent that it does not, the self loses (or fails to gain) its freedom and its power to preside. Symbols make personal freedom possible. They do not guarantee it.

There are dimensions of man's life which approximate the levels of response operative in the spider and the dog. But the distinctive fact about human life is the human organism's capacity to symbolize, and its consequent freedom. To an indeterminable extent the human self lives not in relation to the natural world, but in relation to a world of abstract symbols which it is free to control and, in turn, use to dominate both its natural world and itself.

Before turning from a consideration of the possibility of personal freedom to a description of its actuality, it should be confessed that this preliminary analysis has not established by logical argument the reality of a "presiding self" capable of "personal freedom." What it has done is serve to indicate in a tentative way the meaning of these terms. The unit which follows will further explore the characteristics of personal freedom in the confidence that clarity of description will make obvious the reality and that it is the reality itself, rather than a logical argument, that is finally convincing. Instead of asking what causes personal freedom, we are going to ask what personal freedom causes. Or, better, what are the activities of personal freedom as it overrides its biochemistry and history.

The Qualities of Personal Freedom

1. Self-Criticism

Personal freedom is realized in *the freedom to be self-critical.* Such a freedom is distinctively human and yet alarmingly rare. It is grounded in man's capacity to symbolize not only his external world but also himself. Man is capable of taking the constellation of symbols which designate him as he is and considering himself in a way which is relatively value-antiseptic, relatively free from infection by self-interest, relatively objective and neutral toward the data of his life. This may occur directly as an act of principled self-criticism, or (more likely) indirectly as the self imagines itself criticized from the perspective of other men or from the perspective of God. Probably the latter option provided the original occasion for self-criticism. Particularly in the Judaic tradition, the judgment of God was honored by the historic tradition of men in a way in which the judgment of other men was not. In such ways historic programming may actually function to encourage and support the self-critical work of personal freedom.

But, whether the self criticizes itself from the perspective of God, the neighbor, or some other position of relative neutrality, *the activity is a distinctively human one* in which the self transcends its nature and nurture sufficiently to create a new situation in evolutionary history. That new situation consists in the occurrence of moments of truth for the individual about himself. Following such moments of truth—even when they fail to result in reprogrammed behavior—man is no longer innocent, no longer comfortable with his vanity, no longer in the garden of a naïve Eden. The self, which through symbolic abstraction and imagination is free enough from its own genetic and historic programming to evaluate itself and its activities from a position of relative neutrality, may refuse to reprogram itself by acting from a position of relative neutrality (the meaning of sin). Or, it may be impotent to act on the truth it understands (the meaning of fate). In this latter case the self is sufficiently free to understand itself, but not sufficiently free to control itself. Such impotence may be the result of biochemical or historic programming, and the irony as well as the frequency of this dilemma is the subject matter of tragedy.

But the self which from the perspective of symbolically grounded neutrality is able to accuse itself is also able to excuse itself. It is not just that truth is not always accompanied by potence; it is that truth and potence are not always accompanied by goodness. Socrates imagined that to know the truth was to do it. The Hebrew prophets had no such illusions. They knew that the self may be free enough both to know and to act from the perspective of justice and still not decide justly. But the self which understands both the excesses of its own self-valuing and the demands of justice must choose which of these possibilities it will actualize. When it does so, it decides from a platform which transcends both the perspective of its genetic-historic programming and the *power* of its genetic-historic programming. It is genuinely free, free not simply to do what it wills, but free to will.

For this reason it was necessary to fault as inappropriate the illustration concerning Lee Harvey Oswald and President Kennedy. If freedom-of-the-will is taken to mean freedom-to-do-what-I-will, and what I will is determined by my genetic and historic programming, then determinism does indeed win the day. But if, as I have argued, freedom-of-the-will means the freedom-to-will, to deliberate and decide between symbolically considered alternatives which do not themselves have the power to compel or coerce, then in man there occurs a quality of freedom which simply cannot be contained within the presuppositions of determinism, any more than the flight of a bird can be understood by studying the jump of a rabbit. Personal freedom is a new phenomenon in evolutionary history. Its reality is evidenced in self-examination whenever we do not simply will what we will, but instead, and in the light of self-evaluation, criticize what we will, and will against and in spite of what we have been willing.

2. Hope

Personal freedom also expresses itself in *the freedom to hope.* The freedom to hope, like the freedom to be self-critical, is based on the ability of the human organism to symbolize. An organism that is simply determined by its programming interacting with its environment may indeed be programmed to expect in the future what it does not find in the present. Such an organism "desires"— but it does not hope. Hope is distinguished from desire as a creation of art is distinguished from hunger. Indeed, hope *is* a work of art.

Hope is the distinctively human phenomenon in which patterns of symbols drawn from one's past are aesthetically reordered and projected into the future, and in which the present is then seen not for what it is but for what it might become. For hope the present is understood as (more or less) aesthetic possibility, as the raw materials for artistic creation. In such a situation the present is not so much determining human life as human life is awaiting its moment to determine the future. Moreover, such aesthetic projecting (as hope is) exercises its freedom not only over its external situation, but also over its internal condition—that is, over the personal self's own biochemical and historic programming. A presiding self may take the constellation of symbols which designate a man as he is, rearrange that constellation into a more aesthetic pattern, and then channel the energies of the organism in pursuit of the aesthetic goal. In this way the self (as free agent) may reprogram itself (as historically programmed organism). Personal freedom expresses itself in hope—in an orientation toward an aesthetically projected future and toward the realization of values not yet actual in life and history.

But what is the role of realism in all of this? Is it not true that men often naïvely commit themselves to wishes and dreams which have no possibility of becoming actual in life and history? Is it not true that they often hope to become (or, worse yet, imagine they have become) what they can never become? What observer of the human scene would deny that this is often the case? But when it is, we have an instance of freedom which has fallen captive to its own symbolic creation—and so ceased to be free in the sense of being self-critical. Whereas genuine freedom is free enough from both its actual situation and its own aspirations to be able to judge real possibilities and accept achievable compromises. Even then, of course, there is *risk*. One's estimates may be wrong and one's compromises may be betrayed. But risk is the inevitable concomitant of freedom. Only a determined world enjoys the security of certainty.

The freedom to hope involves risk—and not just the risk of being mistaken. The risk also includes a far more negative possibility. For the freedom to repattern symbols may create a demonic as well as an aesthetic vision, and a man may commit himself to destructive rather than constructive possibilities for the future. There can be no freedom to hope without such negative possibilities. But the risks which accompany the freedom to hope can be considerably domesticated by the freedom to be self-critical, for the freedom to be self-critical includes the freedom to criticize one's hopes and achievements. Neither freedom, however, can fulfill itself apart from the freedom to create—a consideration to which we now turn.

3. Creativity

Attention has already been called to the fact that the presiding self is sometimes free enough to understand itself but not sufficiently free to control itself. In a similar way, a man may be free enough from his character and circumstances to hope for significant change and still be impotent to bring about that change. This is the meaning of *fate* in human experience, and its tragic reality is well-known to every thoughtful person. But, when all the limitations of fate have been fully acknowledged (they will be discussed at some length in the next chapter), it is still true that within these limitations most men most of the time have not only the freedom to be self-critical and not only the freedom to hope, but also *the freedom to create—that is, the freedom partially to actualize their hopes, thus producing the truly new and by-no-means-inevitable within history*. The freedom to create functions when the presiding self commits the energies and skills of the organism to the task of being midwife, tending the birth of hope into the world of fact. Another way to say this is that the human organism exercises the freedom to create when *it itself* becomes the bridge through which aesthetically patterned symbols enter into and refashion the world.

How does this happen? The freedom to be self-critical and the freedom to hope are largely a function of the capacity of the human organism to symbolize. The presiding self is operative— observing, comparing, patterning—but it has not yet come into its own. The central function of the presiding self and its freedom appears in its capacity to marshal the resources of the organism and commit them to actualizing an aesthetically patterned goal.

There is no known parallel to this activity in the rest of the animal kingdom. In the case of the spider the prehuman "self" is identical with its genetic programming, and the problem of authority over behavior does not exist. Already in the case of the dog, however, a hiatus may develop between genetic programming and historic programming or between two systems of historic programming. The dog may, for example, both "want" to chase the cat (because of canine genetics) and "want" *not* to chase the cat (because of training). In such a situation the prehuman "self" is identical with the psychic whole and experiences the distress of competing claims, the triumph of the stronger, and the defeat of the weaker. The prehuman "self" acknowledges the authority of the stronger claim, though it is not simply identical with that stronger claim. In man, however, the self transcends as well as experiences the competing claims of the organism and is able to assert claims of its own. Its ability to make such claims stick, to enforce its authority, depends upon a constellation of biochemical and historic factors. Much of human life is lived—and perhaps all of it can be lived—on subhuman levels of existence, in which the self merely acknowledges the stronger genetically programmed or historically conditioned claim. The freedom of the human self to press claims of its own may remain an undeveloped potential, grow weak from insufficient exercise, or be ineffective due to lack of expertise. Its ability to command authority understandably varies among men and within the history of an individual man. The strength of the presiding self is biochemically grounded and is also biochemically unstable. Both intoxication and fatigue evidence this. The self has powers of "self-control" one moment that it does not have the next. Biochemical technology may develop pharmaceuticals which will tend to strengthen and stabilize the self in its freedom. But the strength of the self is drawn from its history as well as its biochemistry. Drugs will provide no panacea for self-control.

But, if "self-control" is insecure in man, it is almost certainly nonexistent elsewhere in the animal world. On subhuman levels of reality the self does not preside, and presses no claims of its own. It functions passively to acknowledge (feel) the stronger genetically or historically programmed claim and actively to awaken the total organism to its determined assignment. In the spider, feeling, knowledge, and decision are probably one experience. In the dog, rival feelings are known, and the prehuman "self," while signaling the orders of the victor, often also signals its distress over the vanquished (as when a dog wants to chase a cat, but has been trained not to, and instead prances in place). But in man—whose life certainly does include these lower levels of psychic existence —there occurs the freedom of the self to say "no" to all of its competing claims, and to say "yes" to a pattern of behavior which is the aesthetic work of the self's own freedom. The presiding self may both signal and enforce orders to the body which have no precedent in the history and no justification in the interest of the physical organism. In this sense a man may actually "deny himself" (as historically conditioned nature) in order to "find himself" (as historically actualized hope). Or to express the point somewhat differently: a man may choose to abandon what he is in order to create what he may become, and to sacrifice that which is in order to create that which is not yet. That men do refuse to acknowledge the claims of the biochemical organism, and are able to coerce the body they have denied into the service of interests which the presiding self has chosen but which threaten the life of the organism, is one of the great evidences of the self's freedom. The individual martyr would provide an obvious example.

A further illustration appears in the exercise of "self-control" over sex drive. As animals, most men find themselves sexually attracted to some percentage of the female population. This percentage usually does not include all women, but usually does extend beyond a man's own marriage partner. Yet it is possible for a man to define himself in such a way as to distinguish himself from such feelings. As presiding self, he may rule that this is not "me" in love with "them." This is "evolution"—channeled somewhat by historically conditioned ideas of what is sexually exciting—boldly pursuing its prerational and irresponsible policy of seeking to reproduce to the maximum. To say "no," therefore, is not to deny his humanity but to affirm it; it is to exercise dominion over evolution.

An even more intriguing instance occurs when the self, knowing it is weak, and knowing it works better under pressure of public deadlines, cunningly announces such deadlines so as to enlist the service of animal egotism and historically conditioned responsibility in causes which are freedom's own. Thus the presiding self which knows (has symbolically identified) its biochemical and historic ground may press lower levels of existence into the service of freedom. In such ways men exercise personal freedom over their own naturally and historically programmed organism, and thereby modify their historic programming, re-creating themselves.

Furthermore, the self which is free to re-create itself is also free to re-create its environment. The environment of the spider may be different because of the spider's presence—but it is not different from what could be predicted given the genetic constitution of the spider. Similarly, the environment of the dog is different because of the dog's presence—but it is hardly different from what could be expected given the genetic constitution and historic conditioning of the dog. But the environment of man (both nature and history) is different because of the presence of individual men who in their freedom have used the resources of their genetics and history to transform the world in accordance with aesthetically arranged symbols, *the patterns of which were given by neither their genetics nor their history.* The wheel, the steam engine, the airplane, control of the weather, the symphony, advances toward higher levels of political justice, and the submission of men to new truths (sometimes in defiance of their historic conditioning) evidence the extent to which men's behavior and their influence upon nature and history originate in unpredictable freedom.

All of this is intended to clarify the fact that man creates the new within life and history—his own and that of his world. Within the limitations of fate, the self is free enough and powerful enough to reprogram itself and to reorganize its world in a way that is certainly not demanded by the historically conditioned organism or the world.

4. *Transforming Meaning*

But what of those times when the human self—free to be self-critical and free to hope—is nevertheless *not* free to create?

A distinctively human alternative does exist which is different from mere animal acceptance of fate. When a man is unable creatively to transform circumstances, he may nevertheless be free enough to transform the meaning of the circumstances he is unable to control. Such a freedom, like the freedom to create, arises from the ability of the presiding self to commit the energies of the organism to aesthetically patterned hopes. Freedom's efforts to create are in this instance defeated by fate (or a combination of fate and the freedom of others). But freedom absorbs the failure, and in doing so transforms its meaning. This *freedom to absorb and transform the meaning of circumstances otherwise beyond control* may—in spite of creative failure—appreciably determine the direction of subsequent history. Socrates, for example, absorbed and transformed the destructive forces acting upon him in such a way that his death expressed the character and purpose of Socrates far more than the character and purpose of those who forced him to drink the hemlock. Jesus was the victim of despotic politics, priestly pride, and peasant sloth. He was unable creatively to mediate between his vision of hope and the ambiguities of history. He called men to the Kingdom of God, and they answered with the cross. Yet Jesus so absorbed his fate and transformed its meaning that there is simply no parallel (other than biological) between his death and the death of the thieves that died with him. Surrounded by circumstances he could not control, he transformed their meaning in a way that the creators of those circumstances had not intended and could not have imagined. The victim of circumstances, he was free to determine the meaning of those circumstances. This freedom of Jesus was not an escape into a supposedly mystical realm of meaning that despised as meaningless the earthly events which caused his death. Instead, his freedom consisted in the ability to saturate those very earthly events with a meaning so rich that they were hardly able to hold it. Jesus was free to impress upon those destructive happenings his own meaning even as they crushed him, and thus make them the bearer of what they were destroying.

Personal freedom evidences its reality in self-criticism, hope, and creativity. But this freedom to absorb and transform the meaning of circumstances otherwise beyond control is the trump card of personal freedom. It appears in history before the birth of Christianity. But with Christianity—through the symbols of cross and resurrection—it becomes a cornerstone for understanding human existence.

Theology

But what *does* this description of personal freedom have to do with Christianity? Why introduce religion? Has personal freedom *anything* to do with God?

Personal freedom is the splendor of the human animal. But it is also a problem for him. Attention has already been called to the absence of a genetically assigned meaning for man, leaving him to construct a speculative metaphysic to suggest the nature and meaning of his existence. Every such metaphysic implies a religion. That is, every proposed understanding of the nature of reality implies some pattern of life considered more valuable or meaningful than alternative patterns of life. The reverse is also true. Every value commitment or model for meaning (religion) implies some judgment concerning the nature of reality (metaphysic).

A major issue in every metaphysic is interpreting the frustation imposed upon personal freedom by fate. Correspondingly, the religions of the world can all be understood as more or less successful attempts to propose a pattern for life, commitment to which renders personal freedom meaningful in spite of the frustrations inflicted by fate. The successes of metaphysics and religion, like all humanistic enterprises, have been partial.

The prophetic religion of Israel had a highly sophisticated understanding of the self's freedom, but a very poor understanding of fate, with the result that its prophets were largely frustrated and ineffective. The Greeks had a much better understanding of fate, but a very modest estimate of personal freedom, with the result that life was understood in terms of tragedy. Christianity was in continuity with and a development of the prophetic understanding of freedom, but it differed from the prophetic interpretation incidentally at several points and decisively with reference to fate.

1. Prophetic man discovered the reality of his own freedom in the course of seeking to understand his God. Much has been made in modern times of how ancient man created his "gods" after his own image. There is no doubt much truth in this, and certainly biblical theology is unblushingly anthropomorphic. But the development and maturity of the prophetic understanding of personal freedom was the child of a chronologically *previous* understanding of the freedom of *Yahweh*. The prophets believed that God patterned aesthetic hopes for the world, worked creatively to actualize them, and judged men according to the extent of their cooperation. It followed that man's relationship to *Yahweh* was fulfilled and his life meaningful when he patterned aesthetic hopes supportive of the hope of God, creatively actualized them, and criticized himself. Thus, personal freedom was understood as an "image" of the freedom of God—to be valued and developed for this reason.

2. The prophets not only understood personal freedom to be an image of the freedom of God; they were also persuaded that human freedom exists for the service of God. The biblical *shalom*—which is usually translated "peace" but which is further clarified by such words as "harmony" and "health"—was used to designate the aesthetically patterned *content* of God's hope for his world. Men, the prophets taught, are called by God to exercise their own creative freedom in the service of this hope. To the extent that they do actualize new levels of *shalom* within history their personal freedom has fulfilled its divinely assigned function in authentic service to God. Personal freedom is not just a "type" of the freedom of God, but finds its fulfillment and meaning in the divine service. Reasoning from this high estimate of human freedom, the prophets believed that the purpose of freedom was to transform the material of the world, and the purpose of the world was to provide material for freedom.

There is so much important truth in this position that it is necessary to emphasize what the prophets in fact neglected. Namely, they evidenced little comprehension of the extent to which the world may refuse to be transformed by freedom, and very limited understanding of the causes of tragedy in life and history. Prophetic logic was simply incorrect—as later biblical writers saw—in interpreting *every* failure to achieve aesthetic realization in history as a crime of the religiously and morally uncommitted self. Christianity decisively reinterpreted this position by reasoning (from the cross) that even God is in some sense a victim of fate, and (from the resurrection) that a kind of victory may nevertheless be won which reverses and transforms the meaning of what otherwise cannot be changed.

3. With the prophets, the early Christians believed that the purpose of freedom and the meaning of life was to transform the concrete world of nature and history. But unlike the prophets, they were able to find meaning in the struggles of freedom with fate, even when those struggles ended on a cross. They were able to live in this confidence because their *faith* responded decisively to the central symbols of cross and resurrection. Their *theology* did *not* always respond decisively to these symbols, and in the discussion which follows I hope to bring to conceptual clarity their personal response to and the inner logic of these symbols, rather than a reiteration of early church theology. The theological significance of the symbols "cross" and "resurrection" suggests what it means to have the relationship between God and man determined by personal freedom.

Christians understood (as would the prophets) that (1) the cruelty of the cross exposed the sinfulness of man. But they believed (as the prophets did not) that (2) the cross also suggested powers of recalcitrance beyond moral responsibility. ("Father, forgive them; for they know not what they do.") So, with the Greeks, the early Christians accepted the reality of fate ("demons," "principalities and powers," "the elemental spirits of the universe") as a cosmic affliction. They preserved the prophetic aversion to sin, but acknowledged the Greek sensitivity to failure, fate, and tragedy, without unduly crediting them to the sin of man or the judgment of God.

Christians perceived in the story of the cross of Jesus both human sinfulness and cosmic recalcitrance (beyond moral responsibility). But the decisive Christian insight was in the perception of the cross as a revelation of God. The cross suggested that (3) God is the victim, and not just the judge, of human freedom. It implied a God who suffers both with men and because of men. It meant that human freedom has consequences—constructive or destructive—for the divine life. And it is only in the light of this possibility that personal freedom can be finally meaningful. For only if God is touched by the accomplishments and iniquities, struggles and failures, fidelities and infidelities of history is it possible for these to have meaning beyond history.

Against both Greeks and prophets Christians found meaning in the struggles of personal freedom *beyond* both the proximate successes which history permits and the tragic failures which fate and sin impose. That word "beyond" points to the Christian community's confidence in the meaning of the human struggle for God. It was their conviction that man's struggles with fate have meaning beyond the failures of history precisely because God is *not* beyond the human struggle, but is instead *emmanuel*—God with us. Our struggles have meaning beyond the ambiguities of history because they have meaning for God. And, they have meaning for God because he is sensitive to the human struggle, not above suffering and tragedy, and (alternatively) not beyond being blessed by the aesthetic accomplishments of human freedom. Because God is involved in the human tragedy (the meaning of the cross), the struggles of human freedom with fate have significance beyond tragedy (the meaning of the resurrection).

Christians interpreted the meaning of the struggle of human freedom with fate by reference to its meaning for God. They reasoned that God patterns an aesthetic hope for his world, and calls upon men freely to fashion supportive hopes and creatively to actualize them in history. The struggle to do so is the purpose of their freedom. Their refusal of support is the meaning of the cross. (Men's misuse of freedom is God's fate.) To the extent that they struggle but fail the loss is real, but it is not total. For beyond the cross is the resurrection—which is a symbolic way of saying that beyond the reality of tragedy and fate, sin and death, is the abiding value and function of the human venture for the divine life. Men's struggles meet with defeat, and their lives are destroyed by death, but they have a meaning for God which defeat cannot vanquish and death cannot conquer.

This "resurrection faith" meant that Christians could accept the reality and victories of fate without capitulating to meaninglessness (as did the Greeks), and could accept responsibility to struggle for the transformation of the world without identifying failure with condemnation (as did the prophets). Thus, Christianity integrated the competing experiences of fate and freedom. It did so by reference to a frame of meaning in which God is blessed by human faithfulness and suffers because of sin and fate. In the struggle with fate, on behalf of the hope of God, personal freedom fulfills its function, and we discover the meaning of our humanity.

4. The meaning of our life is not measured by our success in transforming the world, but by the effect upon God of our efforts to transform the world. This is the conclusion which distinguishes Christian logic. And *on the ground of this logic stands the freedom to transform the meaning of fate.* Men may fashion aesthetic hopes supportive of the hope of God yet be unable creatively to actualize these in history. Nevertheless, it is not necessary to capitulate to fate's definition of the human situation. An alternative (clarified by Christian symbols, though available apart from them) remains for personal freedom. It is the freedom to absorb the assault of fate and, in the confidence that the *meaning* of events within history is finally arbitrated not by those events themselves but by God, to transform the meaning of fate.

The final height of personal freedom is this freedom to interpret the meaning of circumstances not in their own terms, but in terms of their meaning for God. Considered in its own terms, the death of Jesus was simply murder—a victory for evil. Considered in terms of its meaning for God it is also this, but ever so much more: it is a historical parable showing the continuing consequences for God of human unfaithfulness. Considered in its own terms the suffering of a man with cancer is meaningless—a victory for fate. Considered in the light of the God revealed in Jesus, it is a struggle with fate, in which God shares, and which he experiences as his own. In its own terms war expresses the ultimate depravity of man and absurdity of personal freedom. In divine terms it is also this, but more: war is the anti-kingdom, a regression toward the primordial chaos, exposing the consequences of human life organized apart from God. It is an alternative over which Jesus wept and from which he called men to repent and embrace the gospel.

When personal freedom so interprets the vicissitudes of history it is not simply claiming that the ultimate meaning of events is different from the obvious meaning of the historical situation (though it certainly *is* claiming this). Personal freedom is also transforming that actual, historical situation. It is *witnessing* to the ultimate impotence of fate to determine the meaning of human life. And the concrete, historical circumstances are different because of the presence of that witness. Fate may silence such a witness, but it is powerless to determine its truth. Fate may destroy such a witness, but the witness may conspire in its own death so as to expose fate's lack of ultimacy.

Put somewhat differently, a man who dies believing that the meaning of his life depends upon historical success has surrendered to fate's definition of his situation. But the man who dies confident that the meaning of his life is decided by God has denied fate the spoils of its apparent victory. He has not just defined his situation differently, but in doing so he has changed the actual situation. Fate may destroy him, but it has not decided the meaning of his life—for him or for God. Other men—contemporaries or later generations—may sense this victory of faith, and this failure of fate. When they do—as they did with Socrates and Jesus—the meaning of events for God is felt within history and transforms the reality of all subsequent history. Fate has become a bearer of the meaning it intended to destroy.

5. But to what extent is this Christian "solution" (achieved in the context of the ancient world) a viable option for twentieth-century man? Is not the God of Christian faith—the central model for personal freedom, for whom personal freedom exists, and because of whom one is free to transform even the meaning of fate—precisely the God whom contemporary experience has judged "dead"? Has not this God been found to be the creation of free-

dom—the imaginative work of an uncritical hope—rather than the creator of it?

Certainly *theology* is the work of men. And who would wish to deny that theology has often been guilty of the uncritical embracing of its own symbolically projected desires? Yet good theology *is* critical. And if the very nature of its task requires moving beyond facts to speculations and hopes, then it also requires disciplining speculations and hopes with facts. Disciplined speculation is a perfectly legitimate human enterprise. It is both impossible to produce and improper to demand proofs rather than speculation when the mystery and meaning of reality in general is the topic being explored. Speculation is the proper cognitive attitude toward what is admittedly unknown.

As men, we are able to claim only fragments of knowledge. Ultimately we stand before mystery. Elements of that mystery can be understood. But an adequate understanding of the mystery must include acknowledgment of the fact that there is much that remains not understood. When speculation and understanding have done their best the mystery remains—explored but not exhausted, invaded but not conquered.

The Christian interpretation of that mystery proceeds from the premise that the personal struggle of freedom with fate is a clue to what is going on in reality in general—that a logical and consistent speculation concerning the whole may be undertaken from our understanding of ourselves as a part. More specificially, it sees in the struggles of Jesus with Jerusalem a focus for the struggles of God with his world.

This Christian understanding of God is quite capable of meeting rigorous intellectual requirements. Before the courts of critical judgment Christian faith can persuasively demonstrate its credibility. Having demonstrated its credibility, however, does not establish it as more credible than alternative and conflicting options. No interpretation of reality can produce credentials which certify it as logically necessary.

Man must (and in fact always does) assume some attitude or other toward the mystery and meaning of reality. To embrace the model for meaning proposed by Christian faith is an act of personal freedom. It would not be too much to say it is *the* act of personal freedom—for by it human life is committed to the only possibility which offers meaning to the full spectrum of personal existence. By such an act a man commits himself to a critically examined, aesthetically patterned hope.

This Christian hope in God interprets the origin, the function, and the frustration of personal freedom in a light which suggests divine meaning. Its status as "truth" is as precarious as all theological enterprises. But it has the disintinct advantage of uniting the height of personal freedom and the depth of tragedy—indeed, all the dimensions of human existence—in a matrix of meaning which is impossible apart from this kind of courageous reasoning. Personal freedom can be observed and described, but it cannot be finally meaningful apart from its meaning for God.

II

SIN

No animal other than man creates flower gardens, and no animal other than man fouls the planet with irreversible pollution. Only man is able to compose a symphony, and only man reduces the harmonies of nature to excruciating discord. Man alone writes of utopias, and man alone indulges in systematic tyranny and injustice. Man's technology has shrunk the planet and expanded community with the airplane, and man's technology has burned the planet and destroyed community with napalm and explosives. It is only the animal with personal freedom who can pray "Bless the LORD, O my soul," and it is only the animal with personal freedom who is tempted to betray God.

Personal freedom is both the splendor and the peril of the human animal; it can be constructively used and it can be destructively abused. The hazardous abuse of personal freedom is the subject matter of this chapter. The productive use of personal freedom will be considered in the two following chapters.

Of Sin and Fate

The classical term used to designate the abuse of personal freedom is *sin*. As an activity of personal freedom, sin is something done exclusively by man. Of course, subhuman organisms sometimes act as agents of destruction, ravaging the harmonies of life and laying waste higher forms of existence. Such destructive activities should certainly be classified as *evil*. But they are the evils of fate and not the evils of sin. When a shark attacks and devours a swimmer—making the most intelligent and sensitive animal of the planet a prey for the scavenger of its oceans—it is an agent of evil. But it is such an agent because of its genetic programming (probably some degree of learning experience) and historic circumstance. The shark has done what sharks in such situations do. Its act is evil because it is destructive of a higher form of existence. But the shark has not decided to be evil; it is not a sinner. It is an agent of fate, and the man is a victim of fate.

Men are victimized by fate, but they are also sometimes agents of fate. In continuity with the shark, the activities of men may be determined by genetic and historic programming. Most courts of law acknowledge this possibility and provide for absolving men from guilt under abnormal circumstances of rage, anxiety, stress, disorganization of personality, etc. The destructive consequences of such activities may be quite obviously evil without being the results of sin.

Evil which is the result of fate should be distinguished from evil which is the consequence of sin. Both sin and fate are evil insofar as they produce destructive consequences. Sin, however, proceeds from abuse of personal freedom. It is that activity of the human animal whereby destructive consequences follow not from genetic or historic programming, but from the freedom of the presiding self (1) to arrange symbols abstracted from reality into alternative patterns of possibility, and (2) to commit the energies of the organism to actualizing possibilities which are subversive of the harmonies of life. Unlike fate, there is nothing inevitable about sin. Sin depends upon the ability of the human self to deliberate over alternatives and decide among them. Such deliberation (depending, as it does, upon the ability to symbolize) is not an option for subhuman animals. Of course, there is a continuity between man and his evoultionary predecessors, and a corresponding continuity between sin and fate. The dynamics of both have destructive consequences. But it is the qualitative difference between sin and fate which is important for understanding man. The contributions and limitations of fate (genetic and historic programming plus the immediate environment) are always present for man as aspects of that reality which the presiding self must consider. But they are present as powers to be reckoned with and not as mechanical forces determining human decision; they help compose the patterns of possibility without deciding which pattern is creatively actualized. There is no sin without these contributions and limitations of fate; but there is a good deal of destructive fate which is nevertheless not sin.

Furthermore, human actions which are destructive of life and community may be the results of neither fate nor sin—they may simply proceed from a mistake. A mistake stands between fate and sin. Like fate it is not an intended act of evil. But like sin it is an act of personal freedom. Of course, mistakes can be "convenient," and such intentional mistakes certainly do trespass into the category of sin. It is just this fact which provides an illuminating clue for distinguishing sin from fate. As an intentional mistake, sin is the refusal of the presiding self to exercise its freedom to be self-critical—a consideration to which we now turn.

The Basic Sin: Self-Deceit

Sin is an activity which proceeds from the personal freedom of a presiding self and has destructive, discordant, dehumanizing consequences. It originates in the decision of a free presiding self which through intention or neglect (but not, by definition, through necessity) has failed to exercise self-criticism. This is the first and decisive thing to know about sin. *Sin is fundamentally a refusal to be self-critical.* The presiding self sins when, in exercise of its personal freedom, it patterns possibilities which the genetically and historically programmed organism find attractive, and commits the energies of the organism to actualizing them, but without criticizing its own motives or their consequences from a standpoint of relative neutrality.

All sins proceed from this failure. For example, when a man permits his sexual desires to drive him to marital unfaithfulness and promiscuity, he has chosen to scorn the accumulated judgment of the ages and to anesthetize himself against feeling the wider consequences of his actions. In exercise of his personal freedom, he has, so to speak, chosen to "turn off" the monitor of self-criticism. Again, when a man arrogantly enforces his will upon others, resulting in tyranny and oppression, he is refusing to ask himself the question: "How do my actions look from the perspective of a neutral observer?" He is listening to the assertive demands of the complex organism which he is, without permitting these to be tempered, qualified, or disciplined by the appraisal of a higher, impartial judge.

As indicated in the chapter on personal freedom, the presiding self is able both to accuse and to excuse itself. It is capable of considering itself in a way which is relatively value-antiseptic, as a piece of datum observed from a platform of neutrality. This possibility may be rare, but it is frequent enough to distinguish the human animal. When such self-evaluation does occur it may do so directly as an act of principled self-criticism, or indirectly as the self imagines itself criticized from the perspective of other men or from the perspective of God. The point is that it is only as we permit our decisions to be criticized and qualified from a relatively impartial perspective that we are extricated from the mire of destructive behavior. The reality of sin is certainly not exhausted by the observation that it proceeds from the refusal to be self-critical. But the refusal to be self-critical is the fundamental act upon which the larger reality of sin is built.

This fundamental sin—to be distinguished from the sins which proceed from it—is *self-deceit*. It is a beguiling act in which a man misleads himself. It is a presiding self closing down the monitor of self-evaluation, abdicating responsibility for reflective criticism, and proceeding to live in the world anesthetized to its judgments (or selectively admitting only those judgments which it finds favorable).

Self-deceit is the fundamental sin upon which the sins of the world are built. It is Adam and Eve deciding to "be like God" (and so above criticism), to hide themselves "among the trees of the garden" (and so from the judgment of God's presence). It is every man recapitulating this primordial sin of *Adam* (which in Hebrew means "mankind") by screening himself off from critical judgment and becoming an agent of actions unqualified by critical feedback.

Before showing how the index of human sins is written with the ink of self-deceit, several clarifications should be noted. First, a man may criticize his methods without criticizing his goals. In such a situation, if his goals are evil, this limited criticism may only make him a more effective agent of evil. Hitler probably permitted himself this kind of limited self-criticism (though later in his career he obviously did not). The kind of criticism which delivers a man from sin is concerned not only with methods and effectiveness but also with motives, goals, and values.

The second point to be noted is that self-criticism is not a morbid, masochistic activity. When a man attempts to evaluate himself from a platform of relative neutrality—to see himself, for example, as God sees him—he is bound to acknowledge his strengths as well as his weaknesses. Morbid self-criticism is itself to be criticized precisely because it does *not* present a true picture of a man's actual situation. To be rightly critical is to undertake a judicious analysis of that actual situation, affirming positive as well as disciplining negative dynamics in the human personality. The man who fails to affirm the constructive potential in his life is deceiving himself just as much as the man who fails to acknowledge destructive dynamics. Self-criticism, therefore, does not mean a preoccupation with unwholesomeness; it is just as much or more concerned to discover, affirm, and enhance those constructive dynamics which make for health in personal and social life.

Third, to be self-critical is not to surrender self-determination in order to become an "other-directed" personality. A presiding self which simply permits itself to be determined by the real or imagined criticism of others has surrendered its personal freedom and abdicated responsibility for being truly human. To be self-critical is to *expose* one's self to criticism, to be *sensitive* to its truth, to *evaluate* it according to a criterion of fairness, and so to be *influenced* by it. The delicate balance in which the presiding self exposes itself to influence by critical judgment while maintaining the integrity of its personal freedom may be impossible to calculate and difficult to achieve. But it is precisely this balance which enables a man to be neither a socially conditioned victim of fate nor a socially insensitive sinner.

Finally, criticism always involves some criteria in terms of which one is criticized. These have already been mentioned indirectly, but it will be good to summarize and clarify them at this point. Criticism is meaningless apart from (1) the *principle of fairness*. If a man does not make exceptions for himself which he does not allow for others, and if he requires of himself what he requires of others, he has accepted the principle of fairness and is capable of understanding criticism. Alternatively, the man who considers himself exempt from the judgments of fairness has no difficulty exempting himself from criticism.

When a man is willing to submit to the canons of fairness, then criticism means (2) *imaginatively appreciating the position of the neighbor*. The judgment of other men becomes a valued criterion for self-examination. After all, the other man's life is affected by the decisions which proceed from my personal freedom. He has an understandable interest in my being fair.

But the neighbor may be wrong, and certainly his judgment may be tainted with sin. Self-criticism, therefore, ultimately appeals to (3) *a platform of disinterested fairness or the judgment of God*. In biblical faith God is understood to be seeking to bring all men into conformity with the principles of fairness, justice, and peace. These principles are summarized in the Hebrew word *shalom*, which suggests an aesthetic vision of both natural and historical, personal and communal harmony. To exercise self-criticism is to ask one's self how one must appear before the impartial God who judges all men by the criterion of *shalom.*

Such self-criticism inevitably serves to intensify for the presiding self its high responsibility for adjudicating some kind of armistice between genetic and social programming (for example, between sex drive and social restrictions) or between conflicting aspects of social programming (for example, early religious training in support of peace and a citizen's obligation in time of war). Inevitably, its success will be partial, and on occasion it will be overwhelmed by genetic or social pressures which it is not unwilling but is unable to control. Yet, while man is an animal with only a limited capacity to preside over his genetic and historic programming, he is nevertheless involved in the irony of using this ability far less than he is able, while claiming to use it far more than he is able.

Sin begins with a decision not to exercise self-criticism. But sin does not end there. It is to a consideration of the sins which proceed from the sin of self-deceit that we now turn.

A Short Compendium of Sins

When the presiding self decides to avoid self-criticism its sin can normally be expected to take one of two directions. The first of these finds the presiding self using its freedom for purposes of undue *self-exaltation,* claiming a value, power, knowledge, or skill which is greater than its actual situation warrants, thus disrupting both natural and historical *shalom.* The second direction which sin may take finds the presiding self using its freedom for purposes of undue *self-indulgence* or surrender to its bio-historical programming, claiming a worthlessness, impotence, ignorance, or incompetence which is out of proportion with its actual capabilities, thus abdicating responsibility for natural and historical *shalom.* The presiding self may disrupt the symphony of life by blowing its trumpet too loudly or by not blowing it at all. In both cases the presiding self —by refusing to be self-critical—has failed to exercise its personal freedom in such a way as to actualize *shalom.*

It will be informative to see how these two styles of sin are expressed in relation to some very basic patterns of human behavior. In a general sense these elementary patterns may be called "instincts"—though most modern psychologists prefer to reserve that term for genetically programmed behavior uncontaminated by historical conditioning. In man genetic programming is always modified by learning and qualified by personal freedom. Nevertheless, scholars of the human scene as different as the historian Will Durant and the zoologist Desmond Morris agree in recognizing the universality among men of certain genetically programmed, behavioral dispositions. The following list of these is informed by the content of their work and that of other recognized naturalists. The organization and interpretation is, of course, my own.

1. *The Instinct to Survive.* Basic to all living beings is the instinct for self-preservation. Without such genetic programming life would have been defeated by the risks of evolution long ago. All animals, however, have genetically programmed mechanisms which function to preserve life. The deer, for example, must know both the time to fight and the time for flight. Generally it does—as the result of genetic programming enhanced by learning experience —and that is why it survives. Animals whose instinct for survival (both to fight and for flight) is malfunctioning quickly disappear from evolutionary history. The instinct for survival maintains the ongoing symphony of life. In the case of man, however, the presiding self is free enough to exalt itself over its genetically programmed mechanisms for survival, in which case we speak of *foolhardiness*. And, alternatively, the presiding self is free enough to debase its own powers unduly, in which case we speak of *cowardliness*. In either case the harmonies of life are distorted. Between the sin of foolhardiness and the sin of cowardliness stands a modest courage, based upon a critical understanding by the individual of his strengths and weaknesses.

2. *The Instinct to Dominate.* In continuity with much of the animal kingdom, men are disposed to organize their common lives by devoloping hierarchies of dominance. In the presence of others we feel inferior or superior; in conversation we seek the last word;

in silence we outstare one another; in public we develop a "look of confidence"; in politics we both acknowledge and covet "leadership qualities"; in conflict we openly fight. The net effect is the development of social status or ranking, according to our ability to dominate one another. A simple example from the subhuman world appears in the "pecking order" of chickens, wherein each individual chicken comes to understand its place within the structure of the chicken society. Man's closer primate relatives organize their societies in hierarchies under the leadership of a "dominant monkey," who is responsible for both the external safety and the internal harmony of his group. The relevant point to grasp is that the genetically programmed mechanism of dominance (and its opposite expression, submission) leads to the development of social hierarchies which for the rest of the animal world serve the purpose of creating harmony. In the case of man, however, the presiding self is free enough from these genetic mechanisms to defy them quite radically. When the presiding self exalts itself unduly in relations with others we speak of *arrogance,* and when the presiding self debases itself unduly in relations with others we speak of *timidity.* In either case, the harmonies of life together (*shalom*) can be quite seriously violated. Between the sin of arrogance and the sin of timidity stands a balanced confidence and self-affirmation based upon a critical understanding by the individual of himself and of other men.

3. *The Instinct to Cooperate.* Related to both the instinct to survive and the instinct to dominate is the genetic disposition to cooperate with the community. This behavioral propensity to cooperate is certainly not limited to man. It can be discovered throughout most of the animal world, from ants and bees to wolves and chimpanzees. Indeed, those species which have managed to survive the trials of evolution have usually done so not simply because of their individual instinct to fight or flight, but because of their ability to cooperate in these and other (for example, food hunting) ventures. For early man the tribe, and not the individual, was the unit of survival. And individuals who could not cooperate with the tribe were destined not to survive. The instinct to cooperate with the community, even to the point of individual sacrifice, is

fundamental to the existence of many animal species, and certainly it is decisive for man (who is not individually well-equipped with either natural weapons or natural protection). In the case of sub-human animals the instinct to cooperate assures the well-being of the species. While in the case of man the presiding self is free enough from the instinct for community cooperation so as to be able to violate it quite radically, thereby throwing both personal and community life into chaos. When the presiding self exalts itself unduly over the instinct to cooperate we speak of *selfishness*. Selfishness expresses itself in *callousness* and *insensitivity* towards others. When, alternatively, the presiding self simply surrenders itself to the community we speak of *collectivity*, and note the slothful loss of individual dignity, abandoned for the herd. The characteristic human refinement of the instinct to cooperate appears in what we call "morality." To be moral is to cooperate with one another in such a way as to enhance both individuality and community. Between the sins of selfishness and collectivity stands the integrity of a morally responsible person who has exercised self-criticism enough to know both the reality of his own dignity and the need for community cooperation.

4. *The Instinct to Possess.* Another dimension of instinctual behavior is possessiveness. Man exhibits behavioral patterns which are in continuity with the territorial claims of other animals. For example, the lion's territorial claims have the function of widening the circle of security around the home base and keeping the nearby food supply unravaged by competitors. The possession of such a territory means a kind of security for the territorial animal, while the limited size of the territory provides room for competitors to stake their claim elsewhere. Man, however, is not bewitched by territory. When he lives in a society in which money is the primary guarantor of safety, food, and other wants, he is quite capable of jettisoning any attachment to a particular piece of real estate. What he does need is to possess (personally or communally—"mine" or "ours") those items which will assure his security, health, and comfort. When, therefore, the presiding self exalts itself unduly over the instinct to possess, it may become guilty of *imprudent neglect*

of itself, its family, its community. Alternatively, when the self
unduly debases its powers to preside, its instinct to possess may become transmuted into *insatiable greed*—for objects of pleasure,
power, fame, property. Both neglect and greed are capable of
throwing the harmonies of life into discord. Between the sin of
neglect and the sin of greed stands the self-critical man with both
a healthy regard for his needs and a sophisticated freedom from
his possessions.

5. *The Instinct to Sexual Love.* Sex is, of course, a genetically
programmed instinct basic to all higher animals. It serves not only
through mating to reproduce the species, but in several species sex
also significantly contributes to the development of pair-bonds,
child care, family comfort, and other community functions. For the
hundreds of thousands of years previous to the development of
civilization man's quite considerable sex drive served him well
—chiefly by providing enough children that the species survived in
spite of the high casualty rate resulting from disease, predators,
and war. At the present time the strength of that same sex drive
has become problematical for man. Many of the ancient threats
have been overcome, with the result that the old sexual drive is
there without the evolutionary need for it. The result is what is
known as the "population explosion." Yet, as far as we know,
sex has always been something of a problem for man, driving him
not only to develop pair-bonds but also to violate them. In subhuman animals sex serves to create and oftentimes to preserve the
fundamental unit of evolutionary history—the family. In the case
of man the presiding self is free enough to throw the harmonies of
personal, family, and community life into quite serious discord.

The presiding self which glories in its power to overcome the
demands of sex is likely to be guilty of *pride* or *self-righteousness*.
Holding sex in disdain is the most obvious expression of a person's
rejecting his animal heritage in favor of a spurious spirituality. In
itself such pride may seem innocent enough. But its result is to
separate the presiding self from the biological basis of love. Such
a person may then be calculatingly cold or artificially warm in relating to others. But his life is not integrated and whole. Instead of

responsibly controlling, he has irresponsibly divorced himself from the very earthly realities which an authentic spirituality seeks to synthesize and transform. Of course, such a judgment is not appropriate to every person who is unmarried and chaste. But it is appropriate to certain strands of ascetic Christianity. A spirituality which rejects rather than synthesizes the biological basis for love has largely forfeited its credentials for counseling others concerning the integration of life or the meaning of love for the family and the community. When on the other hand, the presiding self simply abandons itself to the demands of sex, so that human life becomes marked by *lust* and *sensuality,* the integration of personal life and the harmony of personal and community life are similarly lost. Between the sins of self-righteousness and of sensuality stands marital fidelity—the result of self-criticism appreciating our animal heritage while disciplining our animal demands. Under the discipline of such self-criticism sex can be experienced as beautiful; without such criticism sex quickly becomes chaotic, disrupting the *shalom* of personal, family, and community life.

6. *The Instinct to New Experience.* The quest for new experience is not universal in the animal world. The ant appears to be content within his colony, doing those things ants are genetically programmed to do, knowing neither the thrill of novelty nor the boredom of routine. It is not so with man, nor with those animals closest to him in the evolutionary hierarchy. Man is moved by an unquenchable thirst for new experience. When this instinct toward novelty is not being satisfactorily fulfilled, man experiences *boredom.* He is, in fact, bored much of the time. Probably there are two reasons for this. First, man's giant brain is equipped with an enormous number of circuits, capable of handling the environmental threats and demands which were a part of prehistoric man's normal life. The very success of this brain, however, particularly the achievements of civilization and technology, has minimized those environmental threats and demands, leaving many of these circuits unused or empty, awaiting crises which do not appear. The second reason follows from the freedom of the presiding self. Because it is grounded in the genetics and history of the human organism,

the presiding self is never totally without content to consider. But the presiding self is free enough from the content offered by the bio-historic organism and by its environment—even when that content is new—to minimize, depreciate, or otherwise disregard it. Thus man may experience *radical boredom*—due to both the absence of environmental stimuli and the freedom not to have attention absorbed by the environmental stimuli that is present.

Easily confused with the sexual instinct, the instinct toward new experience has a quite different function. That function is responsible for much of what we call "progress" in cultural history: artistic, ethical, humanistic, social, and political. Because of it the harmony of human history is not a monotonous chord but a moving symphony. When the presiding self exalts itself unduly over the instinct to new experience it becomes *legalistic, self-righteous, and boring—alien and irrelevant to the content of life.* Alternatively, when the presiding self refuses to preside, and abandons itself to the instinct to new experience it becomes *impulsive, hedonistic, and deranged.* In either case the harmony of life is distorted. Between the sins of legalistic irrelevance and impulsive hedonism stands creative hope (the concern of the next chapter) based upon a critical understanding by the individual of the gift of novelty and the need for discipline.

7. *The Instinct to Discover.* All animals do not evidence patterns of behavior indicative of intellectual curiosity. But certainly man's closest evolutionary cousins, the primates, and other higher animals do. Yet for most animals what intellectual curiosity they have is directly related to the function of survival: discovering food, signs of danger, and avenues of escape. Only in the higher mammals, and decisively in man, does the instinct to discover begin to become emancipated from the function of survival. This propensity to discover beyond the interests of survival and comfort is the intellectual expression of the fact that in man selfhood has been significantly emancipated from and given the capacity to preside over the bio-historical organism. Curiosity, therefore, is closer to being a function of the presiding self than are man's other instincts. This becomes expressed in the fact that when the presiding

self exalts itself with reference to knowledge it usually does so not by claiming to be superior to knowledge (though it is capable of this claim) but by claiming to know more than it actually knows. Of course, man *is* the most curious and most knowing animal on our planet. Facility with words permits him to symbolize his world as experienced by himself and by others, to arrange these symbols in alternative patterns, to categorize and classify them, and to use them as keys for unlocking the secrets of his world. The refinement of scientific methodology in the past few centuries has permitted man to develop his curiosity in an unprecedented way. Other animals, of course, know things: how to protect themselves, how to find food, how to build nests, etc. But the knowledge of man is dramatically superior both in terms of the quantity of knowledge (there are no established limits) and the quality (which transcends every need of the biological organism). Nevertheless, there are limits to what particular men know. When the presiding self exalts its knowledge unduly we speak of being *pretentious,* and the attitude toward others which follows from such pretension we call *contempt.* When the presiding self abandons the high gift to discover we speak of intellectual *indifference* or intentional *ignorance.* Both pretension and ignorance distort the harmonies of our common life. Between these sins of pretension and ignorance stands man-the-learner, who is self-critical enough to value his powers of curiosity while mitigating his feelings of superiority.

This list of instincts—to survive, to dominate, to cooperate, to possess, to sexual love, to new experience, to discover—could no doubt be extended. But it serves the function of showing how a presiding self which has abandoned responsibility for being self-critical is likely to respond to its basic genetic programming, and suggests the behavior that is likely to follow from that response. The illustrations, however, are *simple*—relating the response of an uncritical presiding self to one instinct at a time. Actually, the dynamics of human behavior are usually more *complex* than this. For example, sex and dominance may become confused—in which case the presiding self may exalt itself in *sexual vanity,* or lose itself in *promiscuous submission,* and perhaps alternate between them both. Again, cooperation and dominance may get compounded

—in which case the presiding self may cooperatively submerge itself in the collectivity of *super-patriotism* or *nationalism*. But the self's purpose in doing so may be to excite a weak sense of personal dominance through identifying with the collective power of the nation. The weak thereby experience inordinate strength through submission. When nations prosecute wars they must count on similar dynamics operative in their citizens—enlisting humility before and cooperation with the pretensions and arrogance of the state. Thereby, personal humility is often enlisted into causes which radically violate humility, and (curiously) men become proud of their sloth.

These and similar complex combinations of genetic programming are yet further compounded by historical programming—so that the possible expressions of sin are endless. But the dynamics of sin—as the uncritical exaltation or debasement of the presiding self in response to simple or complex demands—remain the same.

Given this understanding of the nature of sin, consideration must now be given to other forms of experienced evil: fate, chaos, and demons.

Chaos, Fate, and Demons

Man is a sinner. And his sin is not simply a distorted but inconsequential relationship between his presiding self and his genetic-historic programming. His sin contaminates his community, and contributes to the reservoir of evil (destructive forces) within history. Just as surely, the reservoir of evil within history enters into and contaminates man's own historic programming, distorting the expressions of his genetic programming, tempting and sometimes overwhelming his presiding self, threatening his life and hopes.

The dynamics by which this occurs are widely acknowledged. Man is a social animal. The circumference of his life extends beyond the limits of the biological organism. What the individual does has repercussions for the community, and what happens in the community helps to shape the individual. Man is in his society, and his society is in him.

Man is also a historical animal. The factors which concern his life extend beyond the boundaries of his own limited time. These influences range backward into an indefinite past, and his own influence will reach forward into an indefinite future. Man is in time, and time is in him.

The fact that man is a socio-historical animal helps us to understand the power and presence of the "reservoir of evil" or "structures of destruction" within history. (This latter phrase is Paul Tillich's, and is equally descriptive of both the evil dynamics in nature, such as cancer, and those in history, such as aggressive war). Every sin proceeding from the personal freedom of an uncritical presiding self contaminates the health (*shalom*) of history. In return, the diseases of social history threaten the individual from without and distort his personal programming from within. A sense for this contagious character of evil is not just a recent discovery of scientific sociology. It was well known to ancient man, who had his own insights into its dynamics.

The Greeks knew well the joys of life, and more than any other ancient people they both honored the reason of man and looked for evidence of divine reason in the universe. Yet their mythology, poetry, and drama make clear that they were haunted by a fear that reality was finally irrational—yielding to neither courage nor reason. Ultimately the thread of life, they believed, was spun, measured, and cut by forces of *fate* which could not be explained but only acknowledged. Man was understood to be a plaything of the gods, a victim of their caprice. True enough, heroic individuals could shake their fists at Olympus. But the consequences of such defiance served only to underline the meaning of tragedy: when the presiding self of man exalts itself in defiance of circumstances then its pride (*hubris*) serves only to excite the angry resolve of fate (*moira*). Men are finally victimized by circumstances without and passions within which they cannot control.

When the mythology which shapes this Greek analysis has been dissolved, two points of abiding insight remain. First, by "fate" the Greeks were designating their experience that human existence is in innumerable ways shaped and victimized by forces which the individual person has not chosen. Such circumstances as sex and family status, an effective education, war and peace, and exposure to disease, do enter so decisively into the environmental situation and historic programming of an individual as often to make his choices seem incidental. What is more, it is necessary to ask: are not his choices themselves determined by historic or genetic programming? In the last analysis the answer to that question, as argued in the previous chapter, is "no." But the Greeks suspected, with a sense of sorrow and foreboding, that the answer was "yes." And although they were finally wrong, they were considerably right. External circumstances may cruelly disregard a man's personal aspirations, and internal dispositions may passionately override his personal freedom. The evils which beset us from without and from within are often not of our choosing. Instead, in a way which is beyond the grasp of reason and insensitive to appeal, they choose us. That is the meaning of *fate*.

The second point has to do with insolent pride, arrogance, or what the Greeks called *hubris*. It was in their analysis of such pride that the Greeks came closest to appreciating the contribution of personal freedom to the evils of history. But their preoccupation with fate was so great that they usually interpreted pride as itself simply a product of fate rather than a contributor to it. Nevertheless, pride was rightly understood as inordinate self-exaltation, in defiance of circumstances and in disdain of consequences. And the pride of heroic individuals was seen as—if not itself always a source of evil infecting the community—an occasion which evoked unprecedented evil upon the community from an aroused and angry fate.

The scientific world view, which informs our understanding of nature and history, has replaced the mythological world view of the Greeks. But though he expresses them somewhat differently, modern man has an intense awareness of the realities the ancient Greeks, in their own way, were describing. The lives of men are often victimized by evil forces the individual does not choose, and these same evil forces are often intensified by the choices of individuals. The discordant actions of men make dissonant the harmonies of history, and the resultant discords of history disrupt the harmonies of men. The word "fate" designates these abiding structures of destruction in personal and social history whereby the harmonies of life are made dissonant in contempt of the choices of the men they affect.

A somewhat parallel but quite independent reflection into the nature of socio-historical evil appears in the Old Testament. There, too, the evils of history are explored and explained. The explanation agrees with the Greek analysis in seeing evil as a power transcending the will of individuals, but it is distinct from the Greek analysis in attributing responsibility for the presence of evil *in history* to men.

When the prophet Jeremiah saw Jerusalem, the capital city and pride of Judah, crumbling before the Babylonian war machine led by Nebuchadnezzar, he likened the deteriorating socio-historical situation to the primordial chaos, "without form and void" (see Jer. 4:23 and Gen. 1:2). The Hebrew for these words is transliterated *tohu wa bohu,* and to pronounce them aloud is to sense something of the foreboding they suggest. When the priestly editor of Genesis 1 made use of the same terms he did so in connection with a more visual image of "darkness . . . upon the face of the deep," suggesting the terror of night on a tumultuous ocean. The threatening wild waves of a stormy sea provided the Hebrews with their most vivid natural image of evil, and the *tohu wa bohu* is but the conceptual extreme of that turbulent symbol from nature. When Jeremiah employed the term, he was likening the decay and collapse of Judah to a return to that primordial chaos which preceded creation. For him, the present state of the world was slipping, tottering, falling backward through time—past the kingdom of David, the conquest of Joshua, the leadership of Moses, the call of Abraham —to the desolation and emptiness over which God first began to create.

The Old Testament writers agreed with the Greeks in seeing evil as a supra-human force, threatening and ravaging the accomplishments of history. But, unlike the Greeks, they did not believe that the primordial chaos could by its own power invade creation. God, they believed, had made the world impregnable to evil, fundamentally good. If those foundations were now eroding it was because they had been undermined by men. It is men who open the gates through which chaos invades creation, according to the prophetic interpretation of history.

The cosmology of the Hebrews, like the mythology of the Greeks, is not at issue in this chapter. What is at issue is the role of man in the evil of the world. For the Greeks man is primarily the *victim* of evil. But for the Hebrews man is primarily the *agent* through which evil enters into and infects history. Chaos does indeed destroy the accomplishments and make barren the hopes of men. But, according to the prophets, man only gags on the fruit of chaos because first of all he bit it. So, while the Greeks interpreted life in terms of tragedy, the Hebrews interpreted life in terms of guilt.

The New Testament authors, like their Old Testament predecessors, understand man to be the host who invites chaos into the world. But, unlike the Old Testament authors, and like the Greeks, the New Testament is impressed by the way man is sometimes victimized by evil *in spite of his will.* Its analysis of the human situation is considerably less judgmental of men than is the Old Testament interpretation. Thus, it speaks of men possessed by "demons" (Luke 8:30), enslaved by the "elemental spirits" of the universe (Gal. 4:9), overcome by "principalities" and "powers" (Eph. 6:12).

Today we do not normally explain experiences to ourselves by reference to "demons" or "elemental spirits," and the terms "principalities" and "powers," while less anthropomorphic, still need explaining. Yet the difference in our thought forms from those of the ancient world should not be permitted to obscure for us the reality toward which these words point. Indeed, we have hardly developed better terms for naming the experienced presence and power of the "reservoir of evil" or "structures of destruction" within human history. We do indeed *explain* such realities to ourselves (probably rightly) in terms of natural, political, sociological, and psychological "dynamics" (a word we borrow from Greek which means "powers"). Ancient man had not worked out these explanations. But when we want to describe how we *experience* such destructive dynamics, we uncover a paucity of modern words. It is informative to note how the most confirmed secularist easily slips into language about the "demonic" when speaking, for example, of such a man as Adolf Hitler. If challenged, he will, of course, insist he is using the term figuratively. Fair enough! But as a figure for what? The only intelligent answer is: *a figure for the experienced presence and power of "structures of destruction" in persons and in communities.* Such structures of destruction come to dramatic focus in exceptionally evil men. But they also express themselves in our own personal lives when, year after year, in spite of our resolve to the contrary, we repeat the same destructive patterns of behavior. And they are evidenced in our social history by the wars, injustices, and political lethargy which fails to arise and constructively embrace new occasions of hope.

The New Testament authors, standing in a modified form of the prophetic tradition, (1) affirm the reality of *sin,* and hold man accountable for any contribution he makes to the reservoir of evil in the world. But the New Testament authors understand that that reservoir of evil is filled with a tragic as well as a guilty tincture, in which the historic sins of personal freedom are mixed with what we identify as genetic and other forms of natural misfortune. Furthermore, they take into account, in a way in which the Old Testament writer who coined the phrase did not, the extent to which the iniquity of the fathers is visited upon the children to the third and the fourth generation (Exod. 20:5). Noting the way in which impersonal political, social, and historical trends—principalities and powers—may attack and destroy a man who is not personally responsible for them, but who cannot escape them, the New Testament (2) joins with the Greeks in a qualified appreciation of *fate.* When these historic structures of destruction appear to have made a personal life the nucleus around which their activity centers, the New Testament speaks of (3) *demons.* But whether conceived impersonally as fate or personally as demonic, the reservoir of evil within history is, with the Jews and the Greeks, understood to have something of a life of its own, like a parasitic disease or cancer thriving on the life it is destroying. The *character* of evil (sin, fate, and demons) can be discerned and defined, with the Old Testament, as (4) *chaos.* It stands in polar juxtaposition over against the biblical *shalom*. For *shalom* designates peace and justice, harmony and health. *Chaos* is the antithesis of these; it is destructive dynamics evidenced in war and injustice, discord and disease, leading finally through waste and death to the primordial emptiness, "without form and void."

Chaos is constituted by fate (including the demonic) and compounded by sin. An illustration will suggest the very real presence of fate in human history previous to the contributions of sin. The purpose of the illustration is not to minimize human responsibility for chaos, but to indicate the fundamental role of fate.

That men live their lives in communities appears to be a perfectly natural evolutionary phenomenon. Monkeys and apes are also social animals. But while it is natural for men to live in communities, this does not mean that the particular communities which characterize the life of modern men are natural. Quite the contrary. Man's genetic programming presupposes tribal existence in which his instinct for dominance establishes him a *known* place in the social order and his instinct for cooperation contributes to the harmony of social life. With the development of civilizations (roughly 5,000 years ago) this natural tribal structure was broken down, and replaced with super tribes, cities, and nations. Man was able to override what his genetics presupposed and abandon the tribal structure because of his personal freedom. But while instinctual dispositions can be overridden they cannot be canceled. The abiding presence of genetic programming appropriate for tribal existence while actually living in nations has meant two dangerous dynamics in the life of modern man, which often have for him the character of fate.

First, in the modern nation an individual's instinct for dominance may remain forever unfulfilled. There are too many natural contenders for leadership of the nation and too few possibilities for them to emerge. The results are both a good deal of personal frustration and a good deal of inadequate leadership. (America's free enterprise system *has* given opportunity for many dominant individuals to assert themselves through the market. To that extent capitalism has reduced frustration, rather than having created it, as the Marxists charge. But in nature a dominant's vocation is to support, not just to dominate, weaker members of the society. Many leading capitalists have been loathe to assume this responsibility, and have thereby become social liabilities rather than social benefactors.)

The second dangerous dynamic follows from the instinct for cooperation functioning in a society not organized according to dominance. Men often cooperate with decisions of their political leaders which are not in the best interest of the nation and join forces with historical dynamics which are destructive of their society and perhaps of their species. Furthermore, although man's most conspicuous gift—the instinct to discover—is encouraged by the modern state, man's knowledge is always limited. Nowhere is this more conspicuous and critical than in politics. The limited knowledge of political leaders has the character of fate in a national society and human history which is so complex that while decisions must be made and actions must be taken, the consequences can seldom be foreseen. Men submit to the judgment of political leaders who are supposed to "know best," but who in fact make decisions under the influence of partisan pressure and on the basis of limited knowledge. Each new generation inherits as historical programming and environmental fact bitter fruits of the ignorance, the pressures, the personal and political weaknesses, the frustrations, and the cooperative commitments of the previous generations. It is not just the *sins* of the fathers that are visited upon the children unto the third and fourth generation. It is also the *fate* of power, alienation, ignorance, and social divisions—the chronic infections of every civilization.

This observation should not be interpreted as supporting the romantic fantasy that civilizations create discord and that a return to nature would issue in harmony. What civilizations create are new and different kinds of discord. Tribal existence was a relative social harmony, but one that produced other forms of dissonance. It favored (and was in continuity with) lower levels of animal existence, and seriously thwarted the development of the presiding self and its individuality. In the tribe relative social harmony was achieved at the expense of stunting personal growth—an achievement hardly worth the cost. There is no evidence for any state of nature wherein the various levels which constitute our humanity— genetic, historic, personal—are automatically resolved in harmonious fulfillment. To the contrary, the evidence suggests that contention, imbalance, and dissonance are always already present in human nature. Harmony—both personal and social—is an achievement of the presiding self, not the lost paradise of nature's womb. There are harmonies of nature, but only because nature (apart from man) does not enjoy personal freedom.

The very constitution of personal life and human history contains potential and actual dynamics which are disruptive of nature's harmonies and destructive of men's hopes. These dynamics are part of the human situation and are far better understood in terms of fate than in terms of sin. They may, of course, be compounded and perpetuated by sin. Sin may be an act of undue self-exaltation which creates new occasions of chaos. But sin may also be an act of undue self-debasement which collaborates with chaos already present. Sin creates its own corruptions in history, or it further contaminates the infections of contemporary fate. In either case, sin donates human energies to the cause of chaos. But the serpent was in the garden before the sin of Adam and Eve, and the chaotic forces of fate both precede and run deeper than the corruptions of sin.

A Model for Thinking of God

Two important questions remain, both of them theological. The first is: what are the implications of sin and fate for God? The second question inverts the first and asks: what are the implications of God for sin and fate? The Christian faith symbolizes the answer to the first question by pointing to the cross; it symbolizes the answer to the second question by pointing to the resurrection.

1. The Implications of Sin and Fate for God

The implications of the cross have already been analyzed in the chapter on personal freedom. There it was reasoned that the cross (1) exposes the *sinfulness* of man. It does this literally by revealing man's cruelty to man (in this case to Jesus); and it does this symbolically by suggesting the suffering which sin brings to the divine life (Jesus, in this case, representing God). But the New Testament authors understood the cross to reveal (2) *dynamics of fate* beyond moral responsibility. Jesus' prayer—"Father, forgive them; for they know not what they do"—has some measure of appropriateness which extends in an indefinite radius to all men and to all of nature. God is the victim who suffers because of both the choices of men and the chances of fate. Finally, it was argued that (3) *because the evil choices of men do affect the life of God in a way suggested by the cross, the decisions of personal freedom have eternal consequences and ultimate significance.* Put somewhat differently, evil is finally evil because of what it does to God. When the author of Psalm 51 prayed "against thee, thee only, have I sinned," he was, no doubt, mistaken. Total innocence with reference to other men is an illusion. But the Psalmist had a point. The final referent for our sin is always God. Because God suffers from the sins of men (and is blessed by the faithfulness of men) *the decisions of personal freedom are finally meaningful.*

This third point must now be developed further by defining more closely what is meant by "God." In Hebrew thought the fundamental model for thinking about God is that of a monarch. *Yahweh* was understood to be the king of the covenant people, and the most thoughtful of the Old Testament writers were profoundly uncomfortable about the nation of Israel having an earthly king, fearing he would get in the way of faithfulness to *Yahweh.* Many classical and modern Hebrew prayers address God as "King of the Universe."

The most important reason for faulting this model has to do with its suggestion that God is a cosmic potentate in the Oriental tradition with unquestionable authority. Such a God was thought by the Hebrews to rule his world and to judge his people. But he was understood to perform these functions from a position so far above the tribulations of history as to be essentially untouched by them. This monarchical model was later reinforced by Greek philosophical thought which conceived of God as "absolute," and therefore insensitive to the tears and joys of men. Occasional Old

Testament writers—most notably Hosea, with his model of God as faithful husband—did develop alternative ways to think about God. But the model of God as monarch—who ruled and judged, but was in no sense victim—remained decisive for Old Testament thought.

The New Testament writers have clearly *begun* to break with this model. Making use of seeds which were sown but hardly germinated in the Old Testament, the New Testament writers speak of the divine life not as "high in the heavens" (Job 22:12) but as *emmanuel,* which is Hebrew meaning "God with us" (Matt. 1:23). They speak of God as present in Jesus (Col. 1:19), but also in his people the church (1 Cor. 12:27 and Rom. 8:9), and even in mankind in general.

In the New Testament, thought concerning God is in process of transition from a model in which God is the king of a world which is his footstool, to the model of a God who is incarnate in a world which is his body. Such a revolutionary model—in which the world is likened to the body of God—is often implicit in what the New Testament authors say. Its importance is not confined to a transfer in the geography of God from "up there" to "in nature and history." Its great significance emerges only when we ask: "What is the implication for God's life of the possibility that he is the larger reality in which we live and move and have our being?" (See Acts 17:28.) The answer is that God is not simply understood as present; he is also understood as sensitive to and affected by events in history. What goes on in personal and social life goes on in the divine life. No longer just the judge of human sin, God is now understood as also its victim.

The central event which shocked the New Testament community into awareness of this possibility was the death of Jesus. If Jesus makes manifest the life of God (as the New Testament community had come to believe) then the death of Jesus unveils the suffering of God at the hands of sinful men. War and injustice, cruelty and indifference bring actual suffering and sickness to the divine life. Alternatively, constructive human actions are of blessed significance, and ethical decisions are meaningful, because they enrich the divine life. A man is to be ethically responsible not because he will be judged by an all-powerful, righteous monarch, but because his actions will hurt or bless the life of God.

These implications are neatly packed into a parable, reportedly from the mouth of Jesus, and recorded in Matthew 25:31-46. Sheep (the righteous) are said to be separated from goats (the unrighteous) by a very simple standard. The righteous are those who feed the hungry, give drink to the thirsty, welcome strangers, clothe the naked, visit the sick and imprisoned. The unrighteous are those who neglect such matters. And why are these human activities important to God? Because (God is said to explain), "as you did it to one of the least of these my brethren, you did it to me" (Matt. 25:40). If this analogy is taken seriously it implies that men live within the life of God, and just as mutually supportive human activities contribute to God's life, so the sin and chaos of history are destructive events which cause God to suffer. This means that God is all-present and all-sensitive to events in nature and history. The significance of sin for God is the destruction and suffering it brings to the divine life. This is the meaning of the cross.

2. The Implications of God for Sin and Fate

But surely God is more than simply the victim of evil. Sin and fate may act upon him, but how does he act upon them? What is the significance of God for sin and the structures of destruction? If the cross symbolizes the suffering of God, what is symbolized by the resurrection?

The chaos of the world is that which God is struggling against. The key word here is "struggle"—suggesting (in contrast with Genesis 1) that God is *not* an all-powerful monarch needing only to utter a word to transform the primordial chaos into Eden's garden. In spite of the tendency of certain biblical passages to attribute omnipotence to God, three factors count decisively against it. *The first of these is biblical history itself.* There we see that God must wrestle with an ethically insensitive Jacob; his purpose is delayed by the hardness of Pharaoh's heart and frustrated by the stiff-neckedness of Israel; through the judges God was not able to secure for his people the land of promise; the kings of Israel neglect the covenant and scorn God's prophets; Jesus weeps the tears of God for a Jerusalem which is not committed to the divine concern and not obedient to the divine command. In each of these cases God is understood to be struggling for the creative actualization of a hope which is proximately realized but also partially thwarted by sin and fate.

The second factor which counts against the idea of an omnipotent God is *our knowledge of biological evolution.* The gradual emergence of higher species on our planet certainly suggests the presence of purpose. What it does *not* suggest is an omnipotent purpose. The evolutionary mistakes and dead ends, the sufferings and failures of biological history, show struggle, groping, and achievement. Evolution is a witness to the accomplishment of God —but not to his omnipotence.

The third factor counting against the idea of an all-powerful God is *the theological problem of evil.* The destructive forces of nature and history have already been described. Given this reality of evil, if God is almighty it is hard to believe he is all good (since he permits evil to continue to thrive). Or, given the reality of evil, if God *is* all good it is hard to believe he is almighty (since evil *does* thrive). The classical way of handling this problem is to argue that God is both almighty and all good. He has chosen to let men be free, and their abuse of freedom causes evil. There is no doubt some truth in this. But it overlooks both the fact that there were evil dynamics operative in natural history previous to the appearance of man (for example, diseases plaguing higher animals), and the fact that some human sins have such enormously evil consequences as to justify the intervention of a good God who is able to intervene (for example, the death of five million Jews at the hands of Nazi Germany). Sometimes it is said that while we cannot understand how evil fits within the good purpose of an all-powerful God, nevertheless God does know. The trouble with this theory is that it preserves the almightiness of God by explaining away evil. Evil is no longer evil if it fits within the good purpose of an all-powerful God. But both biblical writers and personal experience witness that evil is evil, and that it is so precisely because it is the opponent against which the power and goodness of God struggle, with real but qualified success.

God is not all-powerful. He is all good—and there is a reason why this can be said with relative confidence. If use is made of the analogy already mentioned—in which God is to the world what I am to my body—then just as it is perfectly natural for a man to hope for vigorous health, so it is perfectly natural for God to have thoroughly good aspirations for his world. This hope of God for his world is *shalom* (peace and justice, harmony and health). The actual situation of the world, however, includes elements of disease or *chaos.*

The presence of destructive dynamics within the divine life raises the question of *dualism*: whether God must reckon with anti-God, and in what sense God's constructive power is struggling with destructive powers. If God is not all-powerful, what limits his power? Probably the answer is "no-thing." There is nothing external to God limiting his power. But just as a city may have only so much in its water supply, God may have only so much power. Since that limited power must be distributed selectively, according to God's creative purpose, it is not difficult to understand the occurrence of structural weaknesses, competing demands, or vulnerable infirmities through which the primordial nothingness gains or maintains a toehold in nature and history, threatening to reclaim creation. The chaos of fate and sin are real, but not as opponents co-eternal and co-powerful with God. They are real only as inherited structural weaknesses and risks against which God, in spite of the suffering they bring, creatively struggles.

That God does struggle for good against the evil of fate and sin is a regular theme of the New Testament Gospels. A considerable portion of Jesus' ministry is directed against forces of evil. On at least one occasion Jesus makes clear to his disciples that the man whose sight he healed was blind not because of sin but because of fate (John 9:1-4). Jesus then claims that the work of God is manifest in his own work of healing. On another occasion Jesus does understand a paralytic's condition to be the product of sin, and he attacks the problem by announcing divine forgiveness (Mark 2:5). Again, Jesus believes that his own forgiveness expresses the forgiveness of God. In both these instances God is understood to be struggling against destructive forces (fate or sin). But his struggle is not an all-powerful one marked by total success. There are times when Jesus cannot heal men because of their unfaith (Matt. 13:58), and Jesus knows well that to cast out one demon may only provide the occasion for seven more to enter (Luke 11:26).

God is not all-powerful. But that is not to deny the immensity of his power. If, as already suggested, God is (by analogy) the presiding self of the world, somewhat as I am the presiding self of my body, then what goes on in the world not only affects God but is in significant ways affected by him. What science has taught us about natural history should also be some kind of commentary on God's power and purpose. Indeed, the word "God" then designates the inner directedness, subjective consciousness, or selfhood implicit in the very constitution of reality, by virtue of which the creative advances of evolutionary history have taken place. This means it is possible to say that:

1. *It is because of the power of God that there is order rather than disorder.* Certainly the order of the world is a proximate rather than a total achievement. But what we call the "laws of nature" and what the Greeks called the *logos,* point to this important fact: things not only are; they are in an ordered way. God is that power operative in the foundation of things by virtue of which they are not simply "without form and void."

2. *It is because of the power of God that there occurs throughout time emerging organisms of increased complexity, rather than a universal simplicity.* The world is not a bland and boring sum of parts all the same (for example, hydrogen atoms). Certainly in that part of the universe we know best, our own planet, reality is arranged in units of increasing complexity—from atoms to molecules, from molecules to cells, from cells to organs, from organs to organisms, climaxing (apparently) in man.

3. *It is because of the power of God that there occurs increasing psychic awareness and sensitivity rather than unconsciousness.* Actually, there is no point in nature—neither protozoa, nor molecules, nor subatomic particles—where we can rule out the possibility of some low level of internal, psychic experience. As a very general rule, however, it appears that the intensity of psychic awareness (or subjectivity) increases with the complexity of the organism.

4. *It is because of the power of God that there occurs personal*

freedom rather than determinism. As described in the previous chapter, a kind of freedom is already operative for the spider and for the dog. But the creation of man crossed a threshold beyond which psychic selfhood was given the relative freedom to preside over its own destiny.

5. All four of these observations evidence the extent to which God struggles with and has made considerable advances against the primordial and continuing chaos. A fifth observation has to do with what is less securely accomplished, but is the present center of God's activity on our planet. *It is because of the power of God that there is emerging among men an increased concern for justice and peace, and a dawning sense of world community—a commitment to shalom.* Such a hope is not yet an achieved reality in our midst, but there is some reason to believe our age is closer to it than was the age of Abraham or Amos, Augustine or Aquinas.

Unlike the four previous accomplishments of God in his struggles with chaos, by its very nature *this one depends upon the cooperation of free men.* God is the free consciousness presiding over but grounded in the ultimate complexity which is the world. He calls upon free men to commit their lives to the support of his hope for the creative actualization of worldwide *shalom.* The achievement of *shalom* is equivalent to health in the body of God, and a reverent commitment to *shalom* is the authentic expression of reverence for God.

These five points sketch in bold outline God's creative accomplishments—from primordial chaos to contemporary struggles. They suggest a God in whose powers we can only marvel. After all, as Paul reminded the Athenians, "we are indeed his offspring" (Acts 17:28). But they suggest a God for whom creation is a struggle against chaos and against the sins of men who contribute to chaos. God acts upon chaos by creating from it, by accepting its destructive dynamics as stubborn raw materials for new and higher levels of achievement. And God acts upon sin by forgiving it, by absorbing it in his own body as the cost of creating personal freedom. But most important, God acts upon personal freedom by providing a context for human hope (the subject of the next chapter).

The "resurrection" symbolizes this creative power of God

which, in spite of every loss to the structures of destruction (chaos), demonstrates the resources to recover from setbacks and to advance toward higher levels of achievement. Just as the cross typifies the suffering which sin and fate bring to God, so the resurrection represents this creative power which God brings to sin and fate. To believe in the resurrection is to affirm confidence that in all things —the tragedy of fate, the guilt of sin, the chaos that corrupts nature and history—God works with the personal freedom of men for the creative actualization of a meaningful hope.

On Sin and Theology

Theology is a risky enterprise. It requires of us disciplined speculation from limited evidence. The theologian is always in danger of committing the sins about which he writes—*presuming* to know more than he actually knows, *arrogantly* insisting on the superiority of his own thought, holding in *contempt* those who disagree. What this means is that theology itself can be a sinful business. It is appropriate, therefore, to close this chapter on sin by acknowledging what the reader probably already knows: the previous analysis is but one man's attempt to make sense of human experience from a theological perspective. In theology, as in every other activity of the presiding self, it is possible to be either unduly pretentious or unduly modest. In one sense every man must judge for himself the adequacy of his theology; in another sense the courts of public opinion are cause for terror; in a final sense God alone knows.

III

HOPE

Nature and time have had a productive marriage. Together, they have brought forth more than one million species of
animals and more than 335,000 kinds of plants. But man is their
most exceptional child. He alone, as far as we know, is equipped
with personal freedom. Other animals appear to be genetically
programmed and historically conditioned to respond in prescribed
ways to stimuli from their world. Genetic and historic programming
also help to constitute man. But man does not live in a simple
stimulus-response relationship to his world. He is both related
to and protected from his world by the priestly mediation of verbal
symbols. Out of this situation emerges his freedom. For, in a way
not dictated by nature or nurture, he is able to take patterns of

symbols which represent his world and rearrange them into alternative patterns of possibility (quite different from the world as originally experienced and symbolized). Such alternative patterns can then become both motive and blueprint for creatively transforming the very realities which the symbols first represented. When such alternative patterns are sufficiently aesthetic, man experiences hope. Hope is the aesthetic patterning of symbols leading to the re-creation of the world.

This means that hope, in an important though restricted sense, is quite literally unrealistic. The content of hope does not simply reflect the situation we call "real." This is not some accidental failure of concepts to correspond to the given. It is instead an intentional act of conception, from which the truly new may be born into reality. But hope is not finally unrealistic. Hope looks at the situation we call "real" and, instead of simply reflecting it, asks the question of aesthetic possibility. Hope considers the real not with awe and resignation but with courage and cunning. For hope the real is the raw material for artistic creation.

Desire, Expectation, Hope

Hope must be distinguished from its correlates on lower levels of animal existence. All animals *desire*. Genetic programming equips them with fundamental cravings which drive the organism toward the future in anticipation of certain satisfactions. In the case of lower animals, such as the spider, in which the capacity for historic programming (the ability to learn) is minimal or nonexistent, genetic programming largely or totally governs actions. Such an animal desires, for example, food. But it does not hope for food. Its desires drive the animal into the future following patterns of behavior which are unmodified by learning and unqualified by personal freedom deliberating and deciding. Men experience genetically programmed desires, but they never experience them unmodified by historic programming, and seldom behave without some degree of deliberation and decision.

Similarly, hope must be distinguished from *expectation*. Like desire and hope, expectation is an orientation toward the future. But unlike desire (which is simply genetically programmed) and unlike hope (which is an activity of personal freedom patterning symbols aesthetically) expectation is historically conditioned. A dog, for example, may expect his master to arrive home at a given time every evening. Such expectation is based upon days and perhaps years of learning experience regularly confirmed. In this way historic programming creates an attitude of expectation toward the future. Man certainly exhibits such historically programmed attitudes. When the buoyancy of animal vitality directed toward the future is sustained and reinforced by learning experiences in a very general way we speak of "optimism." When such reinforcement is directed toward specific possibilities for the future, we speak of "expectations." Man's personal biography and his social existence (including his society's propaganda) create and confirm his anticipation of certain rewarding possibilities for the future. But such expectations are not hope.

Man is capable of hope because he is the animal whose personal existence is insulated from, as well as related to, the world of nature and history by the decisive tool of personal existence: verbal symbols. Insofar as such symbols designate events or entities in the world, they relate him to the world. But insofar as such symbols may be considered, deliberated upon, and rearranged in isolation from and defiance of the events they designate (as when a man envisions higher levels of justice while in the midst of violence, oppression, and poverty) he is in a limited but critical way freed from a simple stimulus-response relationship to the world and related to an undetermined future, to a hope awaiting birth into the world of fact.

Wishes, Temptations, Hope

Just as hope must be distinguished from its correlates on lower levels of animal existence, so it must also be distinguished from its unproductive and counterproductive types on the level of personal life. *Wishing* is counterfeit or inflationary hope—hope without cash value. It is the patterning of symbols into attractive constellations which are, however, incapable of effective circulation on the markets of reality, and which are unbacked by the capital of commitment. Daydreams and fantasies are similarly bogus hope. In such reveries the presiding self patterns symbols in new and attractive constellations, but without the intention or ability to actualize these through creativity. It is universally human to indulge in such reverie now and again. Indeed, the relaxed atmosphere of daydreams *may* lead to the revelation or occurrence of aesthetic constellations that intentional patterning would have missed, but which are capable of and worthy of creative actualization. But the moment such possibilities are acknowledged and become blueprints for creativity, the daydream has ceased to be a daydream and become transmuted into hope.

Hope must be distinguished not only from its unproductive but also from its counterproductive kin, *temptations.* Moral evil is the result of such counterproductive activities; it is the destructive consequences of the creative actualization of unaesthetic but alluring symbol patterns. Such destructive constellations could be called "demonic hopes," for although they are not aesthetic, they charm and captivate the organism. Temptations may be concerned with any one or a combination of the dimensions which make up human life: genetic or historic programming, personal or social existence. It is not the level of existence considered but the destructive consequences of actualizing such considerations which distinguish temptations from genuine hope.

Aesthetic Criteria for a Genuine Hope

And now it is time to examine more closely what is meant when hope is defined as the *aesthetic* patterning of symbols. How is the term "aesthetic" to be understood? Normally used to specify the "beautiful," the word "aesthetic" is here assigned the special function of signifying a "beautiful possibility," capable of creative actualization by a person or persons. But, of course, such a definition is in need of further qualification. Who decides what is beautiful? What are the criteria which make a constellation of symbols aesthetic?

The first characteristic of an aesthetic constellation of symbols, and therefore of a genuine hope, is that it should gather up in itself lower forms of future-oriented programming. A hope is aesthetic because desire and expectation are acknowledged and given opportunity to fulfill themselves in a possibility which nevertheless transcends them. For man, lower forms of programming do not bring fulfillment in themselves, and when they gain undue control of human life, the results are that man is put at odds with himself, his personality is torn by tensions, and he experiences inner emptiness. What makes a hope "aesthetic" is precisely the occasion in which lower forms of programming merge with a possibility that transcends them; they see a possibility for themselves which is not identical with themselves but which unites them in a higher, more complex, and harmonious synthesis.

Sex, considered in itself, is an obvious example of genetic programming. But in human life sex never exists in itself; it is always qualified by historically programmed ideas, attitudes, expectations, institutions. One such historically programmed institution is *marriage*—wherein sex is united in a synthesis of social obligations: convenient, economic, parental. But it is not until both genetically given sex and historically given marriage are united in the higher synthesis of love that either sex or marriage is fulfilled. Marriage vows usually recognize this need for something higher than a legal contract, and call for a public expression of love and personal commitment. They presuppose personal freedom committed to the creative actualization of hope for a mutually sustaining, enhancing—in fact, beautiful—relationship.

The second characteristic of an aesthetic constellation of symbols, of a genuine hope, is that it relates to the existing world as an actual possibility. Fairy tales, undisciplined by responsibility for transforming the real world, may be charming—but they are not aesthetic. Like wishes, daydreams, and fantasies, they fashion patterns of symbols with which lower forms of programming may desire to be united, but which are in fact incapable of being actualized in life and history. Dreams of unlimited wealth, of sexual conquest, of personal popularity, of power, and of religious rewards often fall in this category.

Failure to distinguish between hopes and wishes, aesthetic possibilities and charming daydreams, has led some men, in the name of "realism," to deny the validity of hope. They propose a kind of scientific puritanism which would seek to banish hope in the name of reality, much in the way that an earlier puritanism sought to banish sex in the name of righteousness. But sex needed no justification by the courts of the righteous, and hope needs no authorization from unimaginative realists. Hope, like sex (though on a different level), is one of the things that men do. It needs no justification—only acknowledgment. It is a characteristically human activity, and to banish it would be to lose an important dimension of what it means to be human. Those who would have us live without hope, in the name of realism, are in fact not realistic enough. They have not looked at the real situation with the critical astuteness to distinguish between hopes (which are realistic) and wishes (which are not). Hopes are not to be dismissed because wishes, daydreams, and fantasies are illusory. Of course, hopes are seldom precise, and knowledge of the real situation is never complete. Therefore the creative actualization of hope is usually proximate. But it is nevertheless most certainly real. Hope is an authentically human activity, and it is to be distinguished from wishes precisely because of its realism.

The patterning of symbols in contemplation of the future may provide (1) an attractive synthesis for lower forms of programming, and (2) represent an actual possibility, and yet be destructive of life and history. Therefore, a further requirement for an aesthetic constellation of symbols—distinguishing it from temptation—is that (3) it should be socially supportive and historically constructive, overcoming alienation by enriching relationships. Another way to say this is that a constellation of symbols is only "aesthetic" if when actualized it harmoniously unites both lower forms of personal programming and the human community.

A realistic possibility which enhances personality and deepens community—that is the meaning of "aesthetic," the beautiful mark of a genuine hope. If such aesthetic patterning does not program the future, genetic or historic programming surely will.

Creativity: Overpowering, Cultivating, Persuading

The act by which man creatively transforms nature and history into proximity with such aesthetic patterns is one of the most striking characteristics of human existence. But this activity is in continuity with as well as distinct from the rest of the animal world. Lower forms of animal life certainly function as "agents" which act upon and transform their environment. The spider spins a web (genetic programming) and the shepherd's dog herds the flock (a combination of genetic and historic programming). The distinctiveness of man consists not in his being an agent, but in his being the particular agent for whom the decisive motive for action can be neither heredity nor history but hope. He is able to commit his energies to transforming nature and history in accordance with an aesthetic pattern given by neither nature nor history.

Of course, many times man acts upon his world in ways which are not the creative actualization of hope, in ways which evidence his kinship with the rest of the animal kingdom. Such actions proceed from established habits, which may be helpful, innocuous, or harmful. But it is important to understand that habits are a necessary and not-to-be-despised ingredient of human existence, and a prerequisite to the occurrence of hope and creativity. For habits free the attention of the presiding self from routine matters with which the organism has become familiar. They provide the presiding self with time for the aesthetic patterning of symbols. And when men act upon their environment so as creatively to actualize their hopes, they are not free, and could hardly wish to be free, from genetic and historic programming. (Who would want to have to signal his heart when to beat or direct his leg muscles how to walk?) Nevertheless, the creative actualization of hope, while dependent upon, is not determined by genetics or history. It is the creation of the truly new.

How does this creation occur? There are different forms of creativity appropriate to different levels of existence. Man transforms the realm of the inorganic by *overpowering* it. With a vision of hope and the tools of intelligence, he is able to use his limited strength in surprisingly effective ways. For example, there occurred a time in history when man's biologically given need for warmth and his historically learned knowledge that sections of the earth yielded significant amounts of ignitable carbon were symbolically patterned into the marketable hope that all homes could be warmed through the coal industry. The development of mines was an act by which the brute matter of the planet was explored, excavated, and extracted by muscle and machine in the creative actualization of hope.

Although man may and sometimes does treat the realm of the organic in ways indistinguishable from his treatment of the inorganic, the new dimension of reality does render appropriate a new approach to creativity. Man transforms the organic by *cultivating* it. When man first developed, for example, herds and agriculture, he did so as the result of an aesthetic synthesis of symbols. Symbols designating the biological need for food and symbols designating the historically (and probably accidentally) learned possibility of domesticating animals and sowing seeds were aesthetically united and universalized in a constellation promising hunger satisfied by nourishment in abundance. But animals and plants, if they were to be available for food year round, needed more than overpowering. They needed care. Flocks needed to be fed, and gardens needed to be tended. They had, within limits controlled by man, a life of their own—a life without which they were of no service. The creative actualization of hope within the realm of the organic takes place not simply by overpowering but by cultivating it.

And among men? How does the creative actualization of hope take place between human personalities and within societies? Certainly men can be overpowered, and their responses can be cultivated through propaganda and social manipulation. But such accomplishments are always less than truly aesthetic, and consequently less than hoped for. A genuine hope is creatively actualized among men only by *persuading*—an activity which respects the personal freedom of the other man. A good example might appear in the varied uses of the word "peace." Peace may be simply

imposed upon a people by overpowering them. This is the peace
of the victor, and its reality has been immortalized in the phrase
pax Romana. But when the United States defeated and occupied
Japan in World War II, it did more than simply overpower and
enforce a *pax Americana.* A conscious (and considerably successful) effort was made, through the schools, news media, and other
sources, to cultivate ideological pacifism. Propaganda and social
engineering were used to "guarantee" that Japan's warlords remained dethroned. The success of the attempt has been impressive,
to the extent that today, given significant shifts in the balance of
power in Asia, many United States military authorities judge
Japan's pacifism to be a serious inconvenience. Yet, while this
success of behavioral engineering is impressive, Japan has not had
to face the threat of further military invasion, and genetically programmed belligerence in guardianship of territory has had no
occasion to compete with historically programmed ideological
pacifism. Should such an occasion arise the decisive influence will
be an act of personal freedom (originating with Japan's leaders
but sustained by the nation) in which the presiding self deliberates
over competing claims and decides between them, or patterns a
new aesthetic alternative and commits the organism to its creative
actualization.

This means that the creative fulfillment of hope within societies finally depends upon persuasion, in which an attempt is
made to woo the free, presiding self of other men by offering them
genuine, aesthetic alternatives. The most persuasive aesthetic alternative is the hope of God. But before consideration can be given
to the divine hope, a preliminary clarification must be noted.

Ground for Hope

Sometimes the question is asked: "On what grounds can a
man legitimately hope?" Insofar as this question expresses a
strategic concern to discover the actual possibilities for aesthetic
creation in a particular situation, no general answer can be given.
The possibilities are always particular—broad or narrow, open to

hope or restricted by fate. But insofar as the question is concerned with discovering a universal ground or principle underlying and overriding the ambiguities of nature and history, promising man at least a general support in his efforts to actualize his hopes, the answer must be divided into two parts. Considered only from the perspective of a scientifically observed nature, history, and anthropology, the decisive ground for hope is the reality of other men who also hope. Evidence from interstellar space, biological evolution, and progress in human history, while perhaps impressive, is not conclusive. And this is precisely what one should anticipate. Hope is itself an activity of personal freedom, and the subpersonal world is hardly the place for hope to find unambiguous support. Again, hope is an activity of personal freedom, and that which is a function of freedom is understandably lonely in a world that appears largely determined by cause and effect. It is not in cosmology, evolution, or social history, but in historical biography and self-examination—more particularly, in the activities of personal freedom—that hope finds kin and community, mutual support and encouragement. Men do hope, and they do creatively actualize aesthetic possibilities. Of course, because men are free there is no causally determined guarantee that they will choose the aesthetic. But the fact that men do hope—and support one another's hopes—is the most decisive ground for encouragement *which nature and anthropology provide.*

There is a second answer to this question concerning a universal ground for hope, but it takes us beyond the bounds of nature and anthropology into theology.

The men of the New Testament understood themselves to be victimized by fate and corrupted by sin. Given such an analysis of the human predicament, religion was concerned with the quest for a deliverer who would forgive (or a forgiver who could deliver). The realities of fate and sin have certainly not disappeared after 2,000 years. But man's situation has, nevertheless, changed. Modern man has an intensified awareness of the power and the possibilities of the presiding self. Scientific technology has opened the possibility of doing battle with fate, and social engineering holds the promise of mitigating (not eliminating) sin. In this age of man's awakening power the *controlling* need of human life is not for deliverance and forgiveness, but for a sense of direction which will suggest how that power should be used and will promise meaning for human life. The religious quest that distinguishes our time is the search for a meaningful hope.

The question concerning a hope that gives meaning to all hopes is seldom in focus for the biblical writers—though an answer is implicit in their faith and theology. The remainder of this chapter will be concerned with a theological analysis of hope—more particularly with a hope that gives direction to the hopes of men. The final chapter develops an answer to the question of the meaning of life.

The Hope of God: *Shalom*

It is with a good deal of insight that biblical theology is able to speak concerning "the God of hope" (Rom. 15:13). In context, this phrase means *the God in whom we hope,* because of whom we are able to hope. That thought is important, and it will be necessary to return to it. But throughout biblical history the God of hope is also consistently portrayed as *the God who hopes.* God is understood to have fashioned aesthetic possibilities for Abraham and to have called him to faithfulness. Through Moses God held up a hope for the victims of Egyptian bondage and called for creative courage. Through the prophets God patterned new, aesthetic visions of justice and demanded obedience. Through Jesus God awakened men to a comprehensive hope for the Kingdom and called them to discipleship. This final illustration is the most illuminating because the "Kingdom" is a comprehensive aesthetic vision. It suggests that God holds a universal hope for his world and calls upon men to fashion and to creatively actualize supportive hopes.

The character or quality of this universal hope of God is best suggested in the magnificently comprehensive Old Testament word *shalom. Shalom* is normally translated "peace," and St. Paul, who writes about "the God of hope," can in the same chapter use the substitute phrase "the God of peace" (Rom. 15:33). However, the simple translation "peace" is inadequate. In English (and in many other languages) the word "peace" can suggest the mere absence of conflict—the peace of oppression (*pax Romana*) or the stillness of death. This is not true with the Hebrew word *shalom* (and its Semitic cognates). *Shalom designates the peace of a living symphony,* in which individual notes, discords, and counter melodies are not canceled but gathered up and resolved in a higher, harmonic synthesis. It means a *joyful peace* in which individual notes sound clearly, and in which they both enhance and are enhanced by one another. It means a *cooperative* peace in which individual notes seek not to cancel but to balance and to supplement (and be supplemented by) one another. It means a *dynamic peace* in which the music of history moves on, and living notes are challenged to discover new relationships of mutual support. It means a *universal peace* in which individual notes discover their meaning in their contribution to the whole. In this sense *shalom* is used to designate the character or quality of divine hope, and the hope of God is understood to be for the universal realization of the harmonic symphony of life—which is *shalom.*

For personal life this means "the hope of righteousness" (Gal. 5:5). "Righteousness" is understood as the achievement of a "right" and, therefore, harmonious relationship between the oftentimes competing aspects of a man's genetic and historic programming, or between the hopes of his personal existence and the hope of God. *Shalom* is this hope for a peace of dynamic harmony in personal life. Another familiar term from the New Testament is the "hope of salvation" (1 Thess. 5:8). It is similarly the hope for salvation from the destructive conflicts which characterize personal life when genetic and historic programming, or different aspects of historic programming, put a man at odds with himself, or when the decisions of personal freedom put him in discord with God. It is salvation from the plight of inner conflict described by St. Paul: "I do not do the good I want, but the evil I do not want is what I do" (Rom. 7:19). Significantly, the New Testament word translated "salvation" can also mean "health." *Shalom* in personal life designates the hope for a healthy harmony among the various dimensions of personal existence, and between personal existence and God.

But *shalom* is concerned with more than health in personal existence. It is also the hope for a peace of dynamic harmony in human history. Indeed, there can be no personal harmony amid universal discord. Therefore, Luke understands the good news concerning Jesus to mean angels singing of peace *on earth* (Luke 2:14). Throughout the New Testament this hope for the worldwide realization of *shalom* is understood to be the central concern of Jesus, and is summarized in the phrase "Kingdom of God" (Mark 1:14,15 and Luke 4:43). By the use of a word drawn from the realm of politics—"kingdom"—Jesus designated an aesthetic vision of social harmony in which the lives of men and their communities, nations, and cultures, become dynamic systems of mutual support ultimately responding to the rule of God.

Indeed, the consistency of the biblical hope for the universal realization of *shalom* is not complete until the whole realm of nature is lifted into participation. Paul hopes for the time when "creation itself will be set free from its bondage to decay and obtain the glorious liberty of the children of God" (Rom. 8:21), and Isaiah envisions the competing claims of wolf and lamb, calf and lion, child and asp resolved in a time when "the earth shall be full of the knowledge of the LORD" (Isa. 11:1-9; also Ezek. 47:1-12).

In biblical theology *shalom* designates the content of divine hope. God calls upon men to fashion and commit themselves to the creative realization of supportive hopes. Thus Jesus counsels, " 'Blessed are the peacemakers' " (Matt. 5:9). The Psalmist writes, "seek peace, and pursue it" (Ps. 34:14). St. Paul advises, "live in peace, and the God of love and peace will be with you" (2 Cor. 13:11). The letter we know as Hebrews urges, "Strive for peace with all men" (Heb. 12:14). In each of these cases "peace" signifies the hope for *shalom*—an aesthetic vision of harmonious, mutually supportive relationships within and among men, their communities, nature, and God.

This vision of *shalom* is the passion of biblical faith. Yet the biblical writers were no less conscious than we that the world does not have this *shalom*. They knew that personal life and community life, the relationship of cultures and the affairs of nations, are not marked by harmony. Hard experience taught them that the world cannot give *shalom* to men (John 14:27). The world is full of "tribulation" (John 16:33), victimized by chaos. Nevertheless, they believed men can give *shalom* to the world. Its discord, distress, and tribulation partially have been and progressively can be "overcome." The hope of God and the supportive hopes of faithful men can creatively resolve the disharmonies and transform the tribulations of nature and history. The extent to which men commit the energies of their lives to creatively realizing the hope of the divine life is an index of their discipleship.

So believed the biblical writers. But to what extent is it possible for us—men of the twentieth century—to believe it? Given the evils of history, the weakness and corruption of men (including ourselves), how is such a vision of hope to be distinguished from mere wishing on a grand scale? The answer is that precisely the same "aesthetic" requirements hold for a theology of the divine hope as hold for any other hope. By definition the vision of *shalom* —as personal harmony within a context of universal harmony— unites the divisions of personal life and is socially supportive. (It meets two of the requirements for "aesthetic.") The thorny question, therefore, becomes: to what extent does it represent an actual possibility?

Certainly an individual man cannot legitimately hope to actualize through creativity the universal realization of *shalom*. But certainly he can hope to actualize it partially in his own life, community, and history. Theological hope does not suggest herculean individuals achieving the impossible, but men of hope who will not rest satisfied with less than the possible. It is not a universal vision of what *I* can create, but a universal vision of what the community of mankind can create by commitment to the hope of God. Discipleship to the God of *shalom* does not mean peace without struggle. Discipleship means the struggle for peace, a struggle with fate, recalcitrance, temptations, and tribulation.

Many years ago Reinhold Niebuhr wrote defending the relevance of an impossible ethical ideal. It was his position that an ideal which cannot be simply transmuted into present history is nevertheless relevant in two ways. First, it exposes, judges, and condemns our shortcomings, forbidding us to be satisfied with the present order. But second, it challenges us with the demand that we move beyond our present accomplishments into higher levels of achievement. It is thus relevant to every moment, though possible in none. The universal realization of *shalom* is certainly not an immediate possibility. But the relative and proximate increase of *shalom* is in every moment a very realistic possibility.

Theological hope must be realistic, or it must be abandoned. But the hope for *shalom* and the demands of discipleship are passionately realistic. Of course, a hope is not intended simply to reflect the situation we call "real." A hope looks at the real as the raw materials for artistic creation. Certainly it is true that the cussedness of nature and the ambiguities of history offer little evidence of resolving themselves into the harmony of *shalom*. If they are to be resolved it will call for more than nature and time. It will call for the transforming creativity of men. How is this possible? How are men able—in Jesus' words—to "overcome the world"? That is the question to which we now turn.

Tools of Persuasion

St. Paul wrote to the Christians at Corinth: "we persuade men" (2 Cor. 5:11). But how? If men create among men by persuasion, how do they create *shalom* in a recalcitrant and corrupt world?

In an important sense the answer to that question is always specific, and every particular solution is therefore partially defined by the nature of its particular problem. Nevertheless, there are general guidelines with which the responsible man can approach the problem of creatively actualizing the hope for *shalom*.

The first tool of persuasion is the disciplined exercise of *self-criticism*. Harmony is not helped when one note in the orchestration sounds so loudly as to overwhelm the other notes; nor is it served when that note is so timid as to refuse to sound at all. Humility and courage—in about equal parts—are usually appropriate. Beyond this, a continuous scrutiny of one's own capabilities, motives, and effectiveness—as they must be judged by God—is the first order of business for a responsible man. He who is not self-critical is in no position to understand, to evaluate, or to effectively persuade others.

The second tool of persuasion is *sensitivity*—an appreciative awareness of the legitimate claims and aspirations, as well as a discerning perception of the illegitimate pretensions and destructive tendencies operative in other men. The proportional distribution of these qualities varies greatly among individuals and among groups. Sometimes legitimate claims are hidden in unattractive expressions, and sometimes destructive dynamics are disguised in pious dress. Only by a careful, sensitive listening to what the other man says, and what is implied in what he says, is it possible either effectively to persuade him, or to know how you ought to persuade him.

The third tool of persuasion is *specificity*. The general hope for *shalom* must be responded to with particular projects for action. God calls upon men to exercise their personal freedom in the fashioning of such supportive hopes. This means specific projects in which the individual, on the basis of his own self-criticism and sensitivity, discovers how best he can contribute to the general project of God. In life and history the general hope of God must be transmuted into such specific hopes for creative action. Persuasion presupposes precise projects recognized as possible.

The fourth instrument of persuasion is the *eagerness* to venture creatively into the new. This, of course, is what hope is all about—the aesthetic re-creation of the world. But there are forces operative in all men which make them much quicker to demand change of others than of themselves. *Shalom* is never helped by undue interest in one's own security. Persuasiveness follows from the courage to commit one's self to the insecurity of a not-yet-realized future.

The fifth tool of persuasion is the *maturity* that is ready to accept achievable compromises. This does not mean resignation to injustice, war, poverty, oppression. It does mean acknowledgment of the partialness of one's own powers, the complexities of the human dilemma, and the significance for God of every gain.

The sixth instrument of persuasion is, strangely, the very *magnitude of evil* in the world. The sheer immensity of the problems which beset human history, compounded as they are in our own day by the effects of technology, drive men to ask the question for which *shalom* is the answer.

The final tool of persuasion is *the content of divine hope* itself. *Shalom* is persuasive for at least two reasons. First, the human organism's composite existence as genetically programmed nature, socially programmed nurture, and personally programmed possibility makes man restless, and drives him in quest of both individual harmony and participation in a larger harmony than himself. The ordinary name for this quest is "love." *Love is the aspiration toward shalom.* This definition is true for all levels of human love. The love of a man and a woman is the aspiration toward a harmonious union of otherwise separate lives. The love of parents for children extends this aspiration, as does the love of science, humanities, arts, cultures, and communities. The love of God and his world completes it. Therefore human striving and aspiration discover in the hope of God both a clarification of their own goal and the possibility of their own fulfillment.

The second reason that *shalom* is itself persuasive follows from the first. As a man begins to embrace the hope of God, to commit the resources of his life to the hope of the divine life, *something of significance happens to him.* That something is the partial and passing but nevertheless real experience of the competing, discordant, and chaotic programming of personal life becoming united, resolved, and granted actual intimations of *shalom.* Rival instincts and opposing habits become cooperatively merged in the synthesis of a personal commitment which transcends them—a commitment to the hope of God. Projects which harmoniously unite diverse elements in the world are rewarded by the partial but actual resolving of discordant programming in personal life. The strength of these lower forms of programming is not canceled or ignored but is enlisted in and works for the higher hope. The result may be the experience which Luke described as an angel strengthening

Jesus (Luke 22:43). It is an actual foretaste of the hope to which we are called.

Love is man's natural aspiration toward *shalom,* and the partial but actual experience of *shalom* is confirmation of the meaning of man's love. *Shalom* thus contains its own powers of persuasion.

Today the man who would take seriously his discipleship to the God of *shalom* must seek to persuade men to embrace new hopes for their life together. Specifically, this means (1) the creative realization of *new ways to value and hallow human personality.* Advances in technology, which characterize the past two centuries of human history, have clearly not been matched by comparable advances in morality (the enhancement of personal existence). Nowhere is this more obviously illustrated than in the exploitation of sex for the selling of commercial items such as cigarettes, TV, automobiles, etc. The advertising industry has learned that it can cultivate consumer responses by intentionally confusing genetically programmed sex drive with a desire for the products it wishes to sell. The meaning of being a person—a man or a woman—is often lost (or never discovered) in the preliminary recognition that one is a male or a female. American society is mightily mobilized to tend to our animal needs. But the presiding self—the quality and dignity of personal existence—is the abandoned orphan of our culture. What this means is that we are a society of human beings efficiently organized to serve ends which are not yet fully human. Our situation is comparable to an orchestra of instruments which are professionally constructed, but which are being played by rank amateurs. The prospect for beautiful music is seriously limited. The hope of God for the symphony of life means valuing the presiding self of all men and enhancing the quality of personal existence.

Closely related to our failure to value personality is the social phenomenon which today is called "polarization." It is the alienation of young from old, of black from white, of conservative from liberal, of upholders of law from advocates for justice, of nationalist from citizen of the world (the list is endless). Polarization can be the first step leading to the fragmentation of a society. But polarization can also be the clarification of issues awaiting, even demand-

ing, creative attention. Commitment to the hope of God means
(2) *the work of reconciliation in a polarized society. Shalom* is the
overcoming of alienation, and the achievement of a new, harmonious synthesis, resulting in a more aesthetic community. What Paul
called the "ministry of reconciliation" (2 Cor. 5:18) is service to
the God of *shalom* whose own work is breaking down "the divid-
ing wall of hostility" (Eph. 2:14).

Commitment to *shalom* means (3) *the abandonment of war*
as an accepted fact of international life. This is the most immediate
and obvious meaning of *shalom*. Whether or not the history of
Israel and the history of mankind have occasionally been served
by warfare (and there are impressive arguments indicating they
have), there is *no* possibility of God or our planet being served by
atomic holocaust. This new situation of mankind is sometimes
summarized in the phrase: "War is obsolete." Certainly this does
not mean that the machine of war is incapable of running. It does
mean, negatively, that modern war is incapable of enhancing the
life of either man or God. Positively, it means the necessity of
patterning new aesthetic possibilities which when actualized will
result in a global politics of *shalom*—national communities contributing to the symphony of history and the life of God by engaging
policies of mutual support.

The hope of God for the modern world means (4) *the conquest of racism*. Most white Americans today have some awareness
of both the guilt of their fathers and their own complicity in the
social structures which perpetuate racial divisions. But bigotry is
not the exclusive sin of white Americans. It is a phenomenon
present in almost all human communities—a vestige of tribalism
reminiscent of the ethics of the wolf pack. Recognition of this does
not excuse it. Rather, it points to the magnitude of the problem.
The discords of racism must cause God excruciating pain, and
against them God hopes for the health of *shalom*. A theology which
acknowledges dynamic harmony as the criterion for discipleship
must recognize that all loyalties short of the universal community
of mankind—racial, national, or religious—are idolatrous, and
destructive of the hope of God.

Shalom means (5) *the abolition of poverty*. Both economically and technologically this is easily and immediately possible in our country—the difficulty is political and volitional. The extent to which it is a global possibility—given the varying values of other cultures, unequal resources, greed and human recalcitrance —is a frightening question. Forecasts indicate widespread sections of our planet being devastated by famine in the next decade. Meanwhile, the population explosion cruelly obliterates every gain in world food production. It will be relatively easy for citizens of the United States to ignore such world problems—we have ignored them within our own country. It is imperative that the man who hopes in the hope of God *not* ignore them. Programs for transforming the situation of the poor already exist, and, given creative commitment, will no doubt meet with some degree of success.

The hope of God embraces persons, societies, and (6) *nature.* Biblical theology speaks with penetrating insight concerning man's "dominion" over the earth (Gen. 1:26). But biblical authors had little understanding of man's capacity for *polluting* the earth. *Problems of air, water, and general environmental pollution* are relatively recent discoveries. Dominion is one thing; pollution is another. Pollution is, in fact, the uncritical and irresponsible use of the powers of the presiding self to exercise dominion. Apart from the pressing biological necessity of conquering pollution, the hope for *shalom* means a harmony which does not exclude nature from its aesthetic commitment.

Half a century ago the eclipse of *personal existence* by technological society was only recognized by a few erudite humanists and existentialists. *Polarization* was present in our society, though its distribution and character were different from today. Men still believed in *war* and in the possibility of fighting "a war to end all wars," thereby making the world "safe for democracy." *Racism* was acknowledged, but hardly understood as a problem. *Poverty* was seen as a problem without the possibility of a solution. Environmental *pollution* simply was not yet understood.

Today our understanding of these and other problems includes both an intensified awareness of their seriousness and very concrete possibilities for their solution. This twofold fact is important. It means, once again, that hope is not based upon optimistic circumstances in nature and history. Indeed, hopes are born from the womb of crises, and the possibilities for new levels of aesthetic creation are patterned in response to problems. Jesus' entry into Jerusalem is an eternal model for discipleship to the God of hope. Only as we enter the crises of our time with the determination to discover new possibilities for aesthetic creation do we fulfill the meaning of discipleship. To hope in the God of hope is to seek to persuade men to embrace such new levels of *shalom* within the crises of their common life.

How God Creates

Attention has already been called to the fact that men create in the realm of the inorganic by overpowering, in the realm of the organic by cultivating, and in the realm of the personal by persuading. These distinctions are appropriate both for purposes of clarification and for purposes of action—though in real life they often overlap, and the ambiguities of fate may render necessary actions in the higher realm appropriate only to the lower realm. But if men create by overpowering, cultivating, and persuading, the question surely must now be asked: *how does God create?* The answer is: *God creates by hoping, thereby creating a context for human hope.* Or, again, God persuades men (thus not violating their freedom) by providing a framework of universal hope within which the hopes of men can find meaning and the creations of men can find fulfillment. Such an answer is not, of course, complete. A comprehensive answer would also have to consider the relationship of God as creator to the cosmos, to natural history, and to biological evolution. It is not a comprehensive doctrine of God but an understanding of how the creative activity of God relates to the creative activity of men that is at issue for us. Man stands between his hopes and his creations. The hope of God is the background of man's hopes as the world of nature and history is the background of man's creations. Just as my creative accomplishments take place within the context of the objective world, so my meaningful hopes take place within the context of the hope of God. God creatively transforms the world of nature and history through the creative activity (overpowering, cultivating, persuading) of men. And God creatively transforms men by creating an aesthetic *milieu* within which men's fragmentary hopes find a larger frame of meaning.

This should not be interpreted as suggesting a dualism in which God and world are mutually exclusive entities, and in which God is blissfully above and external to nature and history, seeking from outside to impose his hope upon it. God stands within the world as I stand within my body, and God hopes for the world as I hope for my body. God is the presiding self of the world, who hopes for the world, but who can also be opposed to the world just as I, as presiding self, can be opposed to sickness in my body.

Shalom is the hope of God for his world. Why, then, is there so little *shalom* in life and history? More particularly: why are men so indifferent to the hope of God? Why are they unpersuaded by the appeals of reason? Why are they so content with desires and expectations, wishes and temptations? The answer is twofold. As mentioned in the chapter on personal freedom, the authority of the presiding self is biochemically unstable and functionally weak. Man is often the victim of his genetic and historic programming, and this is what is meant by *fate* in human experience. Moreover, the very conditions that constitute the strength of the presiding self also constitute its freedom. The personal freedom to pattern hopes supportive of the hope of God is also the freedom to close the frame of meaning prematurely, and thereby sabotage divine hope. This is what is meant by sin—personal freedom thwarting the hope of God, aborting the realization of *shalom*.

The cross symbolizes the consequences for God of both fate and sin. But what is symbolized by the resurrection? Given both the reality and frequency of fate and sin, does it not seem that God is impotent? What does he do? We return to the question concerning a ground for hope. In what sense is the God who hopes also the God in whom we may hope?

Certainly God does not throw thunderbolts from Olympus, thereby interrupting nature and history. Whether or not a cosmic bellboy in the service of human aspirations and on call for men's convenience would even be desirable is a moot question. There is no evidence for such a genie's existence, and he provides us with no grounds for hope.

Yet it will not do simply to dismiss mythology and then imagine the issue has been solved. For anyone who chooses to interpret life theologically the question (however phrased) remains: what does God do? How does he create? Why may we hope in him? Can the hope for *shalom* be reasonably understood to be *more* than a projected generality of men's hopes? Does the hope for *shalom* have any real status independent from the hopes of men? On what basis are we to believe *shalom* to be the hope of *God?*

Intimations of the Hope of God

It is tempting at this point to undertake an investigation into the reality of God. But while such an exploration is important for theology, it is not immediately relevant to the question at issue. Even a decisive proof for the existence of God would leave unproven the reality or the character of God's hope. The question at hand is not the reality of God, but (granted that) the nature of his activity.

There are certain widespread human experiences which, when examined with this question in mind, lend themselves in support of the proposals that God creates by hoping and that the content of divine hope is *shalom*. Such experiences are *intimations of the hope of God*.

1. The first of these is the already mentioned sense that my hopes participate in *the context of a larger hope,* that they are themselves a response to hope, that they find their own meaning within a larger frame of meaning. Certainly all men would not volunteer to offer testimony for this experience. But the experience is widespread. There are honest, nontheistic humanists who might not want to call this larger frame of hope "the hope of God." But that point is not nearly so significant as what is implied by the way they in fact live—the way they presuppose *shalom* to be the ultimate frame of meaning within which they hope and create.

Their very humanism proceeds from the "givenness" of *shalom*. Humanists may not explain this "givenness" to themselves as the hope of God. But the alternative is to accept the "givenness" without explanation.

2. Another intimation of evidence for the creative activity of God appears in what at first glance might seem an unlikely experience. There are times in both planetary and personal history when the powers of *shalom* seem overwhelmed by chaos, discord, and tribulation. What sensitive man has not at some time—when hopes seem crushed and possibilities closed out—found the words of dereliction from the cross—"My God, my God, why hast thou forsaken me?"—giving voice to his own deepest apprehensions? The proper response is certainly not a bland assurance that God has not after all forsaken us, or that he has everything under control. It is instead that our very concern for and commitment to *shalom* in the midst of tribulation is itself evidence of the persuasive power and presence of God working through the personal freedom of men. This point is of decisive importance. God creates not by violating or overruling but by working through personal freedom. It is not possible to speak of the impotence or absence of God as long as, in the midst of distress, there are men who have been persuaded to appropriate the hope of God as their own, men concerned for and committed to *shalom*. Living in response to the divine hope, *they* bear the presence and power of God, through personal freedom, to a discordant world. Not just when the world appears unresponsive to the hope of God, but *only when I too am indifferent* have I a right to suspect that God is ineffective. Until then I must say: *even amidst this chaos and tribulation God has done something. He has persuaded me to embrace his hope. He is present through my concern, and he works through my commitment.*

3. Such moments of loneliness are approximated in the personal history of most men. Yet it is the overwhelming experience of men who hope in God that they are not alone—that they have one another. There are communities of concern and commitment; there are *communities of hope*. Men need one another, and never more than when defining their hopes and searching for strategies

to creatively actualize them. We are able to hope in God because he gives us one another—to correct, inform, enhance, reinforce, inspire, and persuade one another. Indeed, unless the tension between the hope for *shalom* and the concrete tribulation of the world is bridged by a community of hope, the strain is likely to reach the breaking point, and issue in despair. It is through the community of hope that God strengthens us. Such communities of hope are certainly not identical with the institutional churches, but the institutional churches are a reminder (even by their failures) of the need for communities of hope.

4. An indirect but suggestive bit of evidence appears when the human experience of hoping for health is applied analogically to God. If, as already suggested, God is related to the world somewhat as I am related to my body, it is difficult to imagine him *not* hoping for his world the kind of harmonious health which is *shalom*. When sick I (as presiding self) am at odds with my body. It is consistent to suppose the hope of God standing over against the tribulation in his world. And just as I hope my body will attain to health, it is reasonable to assume that the hope of God for his world is *shalom*.

5. A final suggestive intimation follows from the very real experience men call the "meaning of life." If my hopes are patterned within the context of God's hope, then they are not ultimately canceled by cosmic indifference, and if my creations in nature and history take place within the divine life, then they make a real difference, and have a real meaning, not just for me, not just for my neighbor, but also for God. The experience of the meaning of life does not "prove" either the reality of God or that his hope is *shalom*. But it is difficult to understand how life could have any meaning apart from its meaning for the God of *shalom*.

It is through this experience of the meaningfulness of life that God empowers men to live hopefully and creatively in spite of circumstances. Optimism based upon the values and creative commitment of the human animal certainly is risky and probably is *naïve*. But pessimism issuing from an awareness of fate and sin warrants neither a general hopelessness nor a desperate embracing of wish-fulfilling phantasies about divine intervention in human history. God transforms history by transforming men. And he transforms men by being the meaning of their lives. The experience of "grace"—of finding ourselves concerned where we were indifferent and strengthened where we were weak—emerges from this intuition and comprehension of the meaning of our lives for God. Without violating personal freedom, God acts in history by awakening us to the meaning of our lives—as he awakened Abraham, Moses, the prophets, and Jesus. When men are so awakened they hope. But that hope is based upon neither a sentimental reading of human nature nor an improbable reading of divine activity. It is based upon the power which transforms and strengthens lives lived in the confidence they are meaningful for God.

These intimations of the hope of God certainly do not constitute a proof. They do suggest why it makes sense to speak of *shalom* as God's hope, and not just as man's own. Theology, after all, is not a simple knowing—though it is concerned with knowing. Theology is the work of personal freedom, patterning under the discipline of intellectual integrity (knowledge and self-criticism), a comprehensive hope. It has neither the right nor the need to claim more than this. Yet as a hope theology is able to venture a claim which knowledge cannot grant. That claim is to have integrated the jumble of human knowledge into an aesthetic pattern which suggests an answer to the question concerning the meaning of life—a consideration to which we now turn.

IV

MEANING

In the chapters analyzing freedom, sin, and hope, reference was made at several points to "the meaning of life." Despite the frequency of its appearance in religious literature, this expression is not self-explanatory, and is in fact confusing. That is because the question "What is the meaning of life?" is a compound question—containing not one but several questions. Each of these sub-questions is intimately related to the other, but they are distinct enough that they can be considered in an orderly fashion.

The Grand Metaphysical Question

Does reality, considered as a whole, have a meaning? In order to understand what is intended by this question it is first necessary to clarify what is meant by "meaning." Consider the opening sentence of Psalm 130, "Out of the depths I cry to thee, O LORD!" If you had no familiarity with the religious, poetic, and psychological use of the word "depth" you would very likely find this sentence puzzling, misleading, or meaningless. Certainly an understanding of the literal definition of depth— as a location opposite to height— would only confuse you as to the Psalmist's intention. If you read the sentence in context, you might have some general feel for its meaning while still not being clear on the use of the word "depth." The point is that when we do not understand how a word *is being used* in a sentence, even though we understand something about the word itself, then that word, and perhaps the sentence, is experienced as meaningless.

Now, in an analogous way, when we do not understand how a particular experience of reality (let us say human suffering) is related to our general understanding of reality (let us say as a creation of the love of God), even though we understand the particular experience itself (this instance of suffering is the result of an auto accident), then that experience, and perhaps our general understanding of reality, is threatened with meaninglessness.

Whether we are discussing the relationship of words to one another within a sentence, or the relationship of particular aspects of reality to one another and to reality as a whole, the word "meaning" describes relationships. When relationships between components are mutually supportive and function together in such a way as to compose a purpose which transcends while uniting the purpose of each component part, we say they are "meaningful." Alternatively, when the relationships between components are unclear, disjointed, contradictory, or destructive, suggesting no purpose which transcends the component parts, we say they are "meaningless." For there to be meaning, every word should have a purpose which it contributes to the sentence; every sentence a purpose it contributes to the paragraph; every paragraph a purpose it contributes to the chapter; every chapter a purpose it contributes to the overall meaning of the book. *To inquire after the meaning of reality is to ask how particular aspects of reality contribute to an overall meaning.* The sentence of the Psalmist may not have been immediately understood, but *it had a meaning.* Is reality this way? Do we need but to understand a meaning that is already given with the nature of things? Or, are there dimensions of evil which contribute no meaning to reality, which are categorically absurd, which function to destroy meaning?

This grand metaphysical question concerning the meaning of reality is asking about the varied spectrum of events which compose reality, inquiring to what extent these events (like words in a sentence) are related so as to contribute to an overall meaning. Thus, if I believe that "The heavens are telling the glory of God; and the firmament proclaims his handiwork" (Ps. 19:1), I will want to know how innocent suffering, or wasted resources, or demonic politics relate to one another and to this overall meaning. And in the absence of a convincing explanation, establishing a coherent and constructive relationship, I am going to experience reality, or some aspect of it, as meaningless.

To ask this general, metaphysical question—what is the meaning of reality?—is to perceive the problem. The question implies metaphysical uncertainty. It is not at all clear that everything fits, that the totality of things constitutes an overall meaning. In fact, man is rather suspicious that everything does not fit, and that is why he asks the question. Chaos (fate and/or sin) is a presence which haunts so many human experiences that some men have acknowledged it as ultimate, and concluded with the author of Ecclesiastes that "all is vanity." But there are aspects of the human experience of reality which do not fit that interpretation. If the meaning of reality is not clear, then it is not clear that reality is meaningless. What is then clear is that our experience of reality is ambiguous. We experience fate, but we also experience the beauty of nature. We experience sin, but we also experience the aesthetic achievements of history. We experience chaos, but we also experience the creative accomplishments of God.

There are certainly aspects of reality—for example, the unshaped gases of the starry cosmos, and the genocide of Jews by Nazi Germany—which do not count as evidence for its aesthetic unity or overall meaning. But there are other aspects of reality—for example, the tendency of biological evolution toward increased complexity and intensified consciousness, and the compositions of great drama or music—which do testify to the presence of meaning within reality. The right question is not, therefore, whether reality is patently meaningless or transparently meaningful—for surely it is neither. Rather, acknowledging that there are incoherent as well as beautiful passages within the book, we must ask: is there an overall meaning struggling to emerge?

The previous chapter suggested that the answer to this question is "yes," and spoke of the hope of God for the universal realization of *shalom*. As *shalom* is a religious and political word, so "meaning" is a religious and intellectual word, both pointing to the aesthetic. A man senses "meaning" when his intellect comprehends the aesthetic relationship between objects (for example, the cells of an organism), events (for example, the historical developments which led to the abandonment of slavery), persons (for example, marriage), and ideas (for example, a metaphysical theory). The following analysis will speak of "constellations of meaning" to describe patterns of relationship among things, events, persons, and ideas (in any mixture) which, like words in a sentence, constitute an aesthetic unit which transcends the meaning of related parts.

If reality as a whole does not evidence an overall meaning which men are able to discern, there certainly are constellations of meaning within reality which men both appreciate and create. The answer which reality seems to provide to the grand metaphysical question is this: I am not yet an aesthetic whole. But within me there are aesthetic achievements. The greatest of these on your planet is man. Man is the animal capable both of enjoying the constellations of meaning which have produced him (nature, evolution, history, etc.), and of creating new constellations of meaning which will produce the future. He is able to appreciate actual aesthetic achievements and to create potential ones. In man, nature enjoys itself and biological evolution has taken charge of itself.

Man's ability to appreciate meanings allows him to discern that I, reality, am not a meaningful whole; in his ability to create meanings lies my possibility of becoming a meaningful whole.

The Humanistic Question

What is the purpose of this organism which I am? It is worth noting that subhuman animals do not ask this question. Man asks the question because in two decisive ways he is different from the rest of the animal world. First, his personal consciousness is sufficiently free from its biochemical ground so that purpose is not simply dictated by genetic and historic programming. Only because this is the case does the question have occasion to arise. The second reason man asks the question of purpose is because his presiding self has sufficient strength to move both his biochemical organism and his world in the direction of symbolically considered, alternative patterns of possibility. If this were not the case the question would be vacuous and irrelevant, rather than existential and of consequence.

With subhuman animals the question never arises. The purpose of a spider's life is assigned by genetic programming. It has no freedom from the control of that programming and no awareness of alternatives. It does not ask the question of purpose both because it "knows" the answer and because it is unable to pose questions. The purpose of a dog's life is determined by genetic programming greatly enriched by historic conditioning. Unlike the spider, the dog is not born knowing the purpose of his life, he must learn it. But learn it he will—he will not create it. Experience with his master, and with other dogs, will gradually program him into the purpose of his existence. He may have some instincts which historic circumstance destine to remain forever dormant, others which go unfulfilled and torment him, and still others which are fulfilled and bring him great satisfaction. But he will not inquire into their purpose. Like the spider, his psychic life is preconceptual —he "knows" the answer, and he doesn't ask these kinds of questions.

The world of genetically and historically assigned purpose is an animal Eden, forever lost to man. His presiding self is an exile, alienated from and unable to return to the secure knowledge of that instinctual garden. This alienation is the price man has paid for his personal freedom. But if personal freedom means the presiding self's banishment from genetically and historically determined purpose, it also means entry into a new world, where the presiding self fulfills its purpose in the enjoyment and creation of freely chosen possibilities.

For the subhuman animal "purpose" means (passively) experiencing its world as monitored by genetic and historic programming and (actively) affecting its world in obedience to genetic and historic programming. For man, whose presiding self is relatively free from genetic and historic programming, "purpose" means (passively) experiencing his world as monitored by personal freedom and (actively) re-creating his world in pursuit of aesthetically patterned hopes.

Of course, man's experience of his world may be painful or enjoyable, and his actions upon his world may be sinful or aesthetic. In general (exceptions will be taken up later), men describe painful and sinful events as "meaningless," and enjoyable and aesthetic events as "meaningful." Two illustrations will suggest how the presiding self—free to regulate its experiences and to plan its activities—fulfills its purpose and experiences "meaning" when appreciating the quality of relationship among things, events, persons, and ideas, and when creatively enhancing the quality of relationship among things, events, persons, and ideas.

i. If I am shown Independence Hall in Philadelphia, I may quite clearly understand that it was in this building that the American Declaration of Independence was signed. But in itself this is simply an experienced fact. If, however, it should happen that I have recently read a biography of Jefferson or Franklin, and if a considerable portion of my energy has recently been spent in exercising my constitutional rights to criticize my government, then I am much more likely to *appreciate* my visit to the historic sites in Philadelphia, to find them "meaningful." I will be able to do so only if I exercise the critical capacities of my personal freedom, discriminate between the revelant historical issues and the irrelevant distractions of a modern city, and consciously relate to the former while ignoring the latter. The point to grasp is that man is fulfilling what we may call the appreciative side of the meaning of his life when he enjoys the aesthetic quality of relationships among things, events, persons, or ideas (in the above illustration, among Independence Hall, the American Revolution, Jefferson and Franklin, and my political concerns). To enjoy a "meaning" is to appreciate a particular constellation of these relationships, noting how they support and enhance one another.

2. The second illustration follows from, and is a complement to, the first. If, because of my appreciation of the quality of these relationships, I should seek to persuade you to participate with me in my attempt to change our government's policy, then I am in fact struggling to create a new constellation of relationships—relationships between the quality of meaning which I appreciate and you as a meaning-appreciating agent. I am also trying to change the relationship between the quality of meaning which I appreciate and the constellation of relationships which form my government's policy. This struggle by word and deed to *create* new and more aesthetic or mutually supportive relationships among things, events, persons, or ideas is what is meant by "meaningful" activity. The point to grasp is that man is fulfilling what we may call the creative side of the meaning of his life when, in pursuit of the aesthetic, he creatively actualizes new or enhances old relationships among objects, events, persons, or ideas. To create a "meaning" is to actualize a new, more aesthetic constellation of relationships.

The purpose of man's life is realized in the discriminate choices of personal freedom to appreciate and to preside over limited aspects of nature and history. In man, evolution has produced an animal capable of appreciating the natural and historical relationships which collectively compose and support his life and world, and who is uniquely equipped to create new as well as enhance established relationships. *"Meaning" is a word which describes the aesthetic quality of relationships within particular constellations of natural or historical things, events, persons, or ideas.* Man is the meaning-appreciating, meaning-creating animal, and the purpose of his life is fulfilled in the appreciation and creation of meaning.

The Theological Question

Who assigned me this purpose? For whom does my fulfilling this purpose mean anything? Have I a meaning beyond myself?

When man asks these questions he does so *both* because the answers are not obvious (thus requiring theological courage) and because he senses that there *are* answers which are both true and rewarding (thus delivering him from skepticism and cynicism). He senses this because he is himself a conscious appreciating-and-creating nodule of relationships within the expanding network of relationships which is family and friends, human society, history, nature, ultimate reality. Each person is a unique center within this network, a self-conscious intersection toward which relationships converge and from which they radiate. When a man appreciates these relationships, and when he creatively enhances them, his activity as a subordinate matrix-of-meaning has implications for the whole.

Interpreted theologically, this means that each man is a subordinate structure within reality, perceiving in a fragmentary way the relationship of the structures which compose him, and his relationship to the larger structures (society, history, nature, God) that support him. Reformation theology spoke of the meaning of human life in terms of enjoying and glorifying God (*Westminster Shorter Catechism,* Answer 1). The whole of the preceding analysis is intended to clarify what it means to enjoy and to glorify him. For the appreciation of meaning is nothing less than the enjoyment of related structures of which God is the constitutive ground, and the creation or expansion of meaning is nothing less than the glorification of God by enhancing and enriching the relationship of structures which collectively constitute the divine life. Another way to say this is that man enjoys in his fragmentary way his limited perceptions of meaning, of which God is the creative foundation, and God enjoys in his universal way the total perception of meaning, of which each man is a creative fragment.

Man enjoys and glorifies God when he appreciates and contributes to the growth of aesthetic relationships among objects, events, persons, and ideas. Indeed, every dimension of human experience is potential material for the appreciation of meaning and of the God who is the ground of meaning. Consciousness of the anatomy of one's own personality, the forces and feelings operative in other men, the possibilities and limitations of politics, the dynamics and disruptions of history, the empirical facts of natural science, and the underlying structures of ultimate reality (God)—all these enhance a man's appreciation of the relationships which make the actual world aesthetic, and all deepen his experience of meaning. But man is constituted in such a way that he is not permitted for long to enjoy such relationships without contributing to their enrichment by the creative actualization of new aesthetic possibilities. Therefore, the discipline of one's own personality, sympathetic cooperation with the legitimate aspirations of other men, the regulation of politics to broaden community, collaboration with the constructive dynamics of history, translation of the knowledge gained by natural science into humanistically oriented technology, and a pervading responsiveness to the hope of God—all these glorify God by augmenting the relationships which collectively compose *his* meaningful world. Each person is a subordinate nucleus of meaning who may appreciate the divine depth of meaning and contribute to divine enrichment.

The Practical Question: Appreciating Meaning

How can I more fully appreciate the meaning present in the world?

Man stands between that which has been and that which will be. The meaning of his life is fulfilled in the appreciation of that received from the past and in the creation of that hoped for the future. The lives of some men are governed by nostalgia for that which has been and fear of that which could be—they are conservatives. The lives of other men are governed by preoccupation with that which ought to be and indifference or hatred for that which is—they are revolutionaries. Both miss the full experience of being human. Their lives are only surpassed in emptiness by those who know neither the holiness of that which has been nor the holiness of that which ought to be.

Of course, all of that received from the past is not aesthetic, and can and should not be appreciated. Similarly, all of that possible for the future is not aesthetic, and can and should not be creatively actualized. The presiding self, in exercise of its personal freedom, and particularly its critical talents, must make judgments concerning the more and less aesthetic, acknowledge real distinctions, deliberate and decide. In doing so the presiding self relates to and participates in aesthetic values from the past or for the future and fulfills the meaning of human life. We must now raise the very practical questions: *"How can I more fully appreciate meanings?"* and (in the next section) *"How can I more adequately create meanings?"* In an important sense every man must write his own answer to these questions, based on a consideration of his own talents and his situation in life. But the following guidelines may prove helpful.

Because the life of the human animal is so largely intellectual he cannot appreciate the relationship of things, events, persons, or ideas without knowledge and understanding. Because he is an animal, however, he needs more than understanding—he needs to experience, sympathize, participate, relate. The balance is important, and will be presupposed in the following suggestions.

NATURE: Man is a part of nature, and (particularly the city-dweller) needs to rediscover his kinship with it. The Old Testament speaks of Adam (mankind) being appointed to till the ground, and the New Testament evidences Jesus' appreciation of nature in many parables. Gardening, in a plot ever so small, can help a man experience the joy of union with that grand network of relationships between atoms and molecules, soil and cells, which brings forth and sustains life. As he increasingly understands the chemistry and practices the appropriate care a man will *appreciate* his relationship to nature and find it meaningful. Of course, gardening is not the only way of relating to and appreciating nature. Astronomy, geology, wine making, animal care, bird watching, and a mother's nursing of her infant (the list is open) provide other possibilities for relationships with nature, which make life more appreciably meaningful.

HISTORY: Few men can become general historians. But every man can and should study in depth some segment of history. Old Testament writers knew the exodus best, and the early church was concerned with the life of Jesus. But every piece of history contains intrinsic rewards, and those without scholarly tools may find access to more recent history practical and relevant. By learning the cultural issues and political dynamics, the philosophy of life and the biography of leading figures from one period of history a man gains intensified awareness of and perspective on what it means to live in his own time. He sympathizes with the goals, rejoices over the accomplishments, suffers from the failures, and becomes indignant over the evils of men. He learns that life is struggle. Most of all, he appreciates what it means to be a man and related to the human enterprise. History helps him to see himself and his relationship to those before him. Thereby life becomes appreciably meaningful.

GEOGRAPHY: One of the most rewarding facts of modern life is the widespread opportunity for travel. It is a point not to be missed that biblical history begins with the travels of Abraham and ends with the travels of St. Paul. Even a few weeks in a different section of the planet, tasting and smelling, looking and listening, can fill a man with appreciation for the rich spectrum of cultures which his fellowmen have developed (usually directly affected by land and climate). The most fragmentary contacts with other peoples, their language, their fears, hopes, accomplishments, and values, make a man conscious of a depth of meaningful relationships he has only begun to fathom. It even excites him to better fathom his own culture. Travel helps man to see himself and his relationship to those beside him. Thereby life becomes more appreciably meaningful.

DRAMA: The theatre can be a revelation of meaning. Probably no human enterprise more effectively awakens us to dynamics and dimensions of human personality. The playwright creates characters which are models of ourselves, and then conspires with them to expose the quality of our own relationships to objects and events, persons and ideas. It was the Greeks who perfected theatrical drama. But the biblical writers demonstrate high dramatic skills in storytelling, and Israel reenacted the exodus at Passover. Ancient peoples knew the importance of drama for helping men feel deeply the meaning of great events and truths. He who appreciates drama is sensing through imaginative participation the dynamic meanings which make life tragic or comic, foolish or wise, empty or fulfilled. He is able to appreciate even the tragic, foolish, and empty because he sees, in a way in which the characters of the drama sometimes do not, alternatives which they could have chosen. Relating through the theatre to the rich spectrum of human possibilities makes life more appreciably meaningful.

ART: Israel's skills with painting and sculpture must have been seriously limited by the Mosaic prohibition against graven images. Her appreciation of music is referred to frequently, and her love of poetry is evidenced throughout the Bible—most majestically in the Psalms and prophets. All forms of art—poetry, painting, music, dance—take concentration to create and demand concentration to appreciate. The factual knowledge, the feel for human emotions, the sense for aesthetic synthesis, the discipline and talent, which goes into a symphony, cannot be casually appreciated. But he who learns to appreciate a symphony enjoys a network of relationships among composer, musicians, instruments, sounds, and conductor, which is a lucid model for enjoying the meaning present in all of life.

FRIENDSHIP: Jesus and his disciples provide an illuminating model for friendship. That model makes clear that persons are the most rewarding source of appreciative meaning to other persons. Even the individual who experiences his own life as empty can become a rich source of meaning to someone else (perhaps just by confessing his own sense of emptiness). It is when we share with one another our hopes and fears, memories and loves, joys and sorrows, appreciations and powers, that life becomes appreciatively meaningful and meaningfully transformed. We establish relationships with and relationships for one another which make life qualitatively richer. It is possible for men to be boring—but only when they refuse to exercise their abilities as presiding selves, seeking to appreciate their world and aesthetically to re-create it. Friendship with other men—discovering their relationship to things, events, other persons, and ideas—is the richest source of appreciative meaning.

PLAY: Wasting time is a very different thing from play. Play can be confused with wasting time because it is not productive of something beyond itself (as the gardener produces vegetables or the artist a picture). But play is distinguished from wasting time precisely because it is the enjoyment of relationships for their own sake, rather than indifference to them. Play is the sheer enjoyment of relationships among objects, events, persons, and ideas in various, established combinations. This is true whether these relationships are highly formal (as with the rules of chess) or informal (as when a parent plays with his children), and it is true whether the relationships are largely conceptual (as in bridge) or largely physical (as in basketball). Play is the conscious enjoyment of relationships for their own sake—wherein the question of meaning beyond the meaning of the play itself is intentionally suspended. The Greeks appear to have had a much more highly developed appreciation of play than did Israel (although the Hebrew text of the Old Testament is filled with puns or play upon words).

WORK: All labor is not meaningful activity. Mere toil may be unproductive or even counterproductive drudgery. The word "work" should be reserved for constructive and meaningful labor. So defined, work is primarily a creative rather than an appreciative activity. But work can also be a rewarding source of appreciative meaning. If through work human hopes become creatively actualized, and take their place among the structures of meaning which enrich history, a man is able to look back at his accomplishments with deep satisfaction. He is able to enjoy his personal relationship to and responsibility for these constellations of meaning, and their relationship to constellations of meaning achieved by others, whom he may also know and also appreciate. Work holds a unique place among the activities of men because of this double significance:

through work a person experiences meaning by *appreciating* what he has *created*.

AUTOBIOGRAPHY: A critically important source of qualitative meaning is enjoyed when a person reflects upon the relationship between who he is and who he was some years ago. For this reason it is unfortunate that most people today do not keep diaries. Diaries help us to see where we are in the perspective of where we have been, marking consistency and growth as well as reverses and transformation, recording our creative accomplishments and instructing us regarding our failures. Autobiography helps us to appreciate the rich network of relationships with things, events, persons, and ideas, which help make us who we are, and help make who we are meaningful.

RELIGION: Religion is commitment to a pattern of life judged to make human existence meaningful. In the Christian religion God is understood to be the ground and goal of that meaning; it is he "from whom are all things and for whom we exist" (1 Cor. 8:6). But no absolute distinction is made between the world and God, between the secular and the sacred—except that the secular is penultimate and the sacred ultimate. Every secular meaning is related to the sacred, can mediate the sacred, and has meaning for the sacred. Good religion includes the conscious enjoyment of the divine depth to which all relationships with objects, events, persons, and ideas are ultimately related. A man enjoys God when he enjoys the depth of meaning in which the meanings present in nature, history, geography, drama, art, friendship, play, work, and personal life are ultimately grounded. In God all lines of relationship meet, and all meanings find their Meaning.

The Practical Question: Creating Meaning

How can I effectively create a more meaningful world?

The analysis of ways to appreciate meaning ended with a brief consideration of religion. This analysis of effectively enhancing meaning must begin and end with religion. Meanings can be rather innocently appreciated apart from their meaning for God. But meanings created apart from their meaning for God can be demonic (as were the blood and soil meanings of Nazi Germany). The answer to appreciating meaning was given in the indicative. The answer to creating meaning must be in the imperative. The former was a matter of analysis. The latter is a matter of passion. That was a matter of theology. This is a matter of discipleship.

In terms of analysis, however, the answer to the question "How can I effectively create meaning?" is largely identical with the answer suggested to the question "How can I persuade men to embrace the hope of God?" (pages 84-87). The creative actualization of *shalom* simply *is* the enhancement of the meaningful world. To create meaning is to establish aesthetic relationships among objects, events, persons, and ideas—and this is what *shalom* means. To thus understand what *shalom* means, however, is not just to comprehend an aesthetic ideal. It is to sense one's self commissioned to discipleship by the hope of God.

It is a striking feature of the New Testament narrative about Jesus that he—much to the consternation of those round about him—actually enjoyed and intentionally created personal relationships with people largely unrelated to anyone, with tax collectors, harlots, and sinners (Luke 7:33-34). Jesus established community where before there was only alienation. He shared with the hungry, befriended the lonely, helped the sick, and gave hope to those in despair. There intersected in Jesus a network of human relationships so rich in character that those associated with him sensed something of the depth and divine quality of the total complex of relationships in which both Jesus and they were ultimately grounded. Contact with Jesus prompted them into awareness of the presence and reality of God in the depths of their own lives. He brought men into the richness of his fellowship and called upon them to be his disciples and join in seeking the fulfillment of the hope of God.

But if the meaning of life is realized in commitment to the struggle to actualize *shalom* among men, it is necessary to acknowledge with utter realism the situation of estrangement, meaninglessness, and chaos which this work presupposes. Nowhere is this tragic, estranged, and chaotic character of human life and history so dramatically clarified as in the New Testament. Deserted by his friends, alienated from his people, the victim of despotic politics and priestly intrigue, Jesus was able to walk into the very jaws of death because he could appreciate meanings (in this case his relationship to God and to the history of Israel) in the most meaningless circumstances (meaningless because the relationship of Jesus to the authorities and to the populace of Jerusalem had more the character of a disjunction).

No serious theology can long ignore this chaotic, tragic, disjunctive character of human existence. Actual circumstances historically following one another (for example, innocent suffering at the hands of evil men) can be the chaotic work of fate and sin, rather than the meaningful work of constructive forces. They are then rightly described as "meaningless" because their unaesthetic relationship is such as to be destructive of relationships (and therefore of meanings). They are "structures of destruction," or what the New Testament called "demons," "principalities," and "powers." Such unaesthetic relationships cannot be appreciatively enjoyed, do not enhance the meaningful world, and do not glorify God. But *they do have a quasi-significance, for they are the Jerusalem which Jesus entered and the unreconciled world to which his disciples are called*—called to change the actual situation in such a way that genuine relationships can be established, *shalom* enjoyed, and future meanings made possible.

This is the answer to the critically important question: how can I participate in the creation of meaning? When a man asks such a question with existential seriousness, when he experiences the historical events which surround him as meaningless, or even as destructive of meaning, he is called upon by God and fulfills the meaning of his life by vigorously entering that situation as an agent of *shalom*—that is, by using the resources of his life to change the character of historical life, transforming the destructive, unaesthetic relationships into genuine, supportive relationships. *To this extent even meaninglessness is meaningful*—it is the very stuff out of which new meanings are created; it is the desert waiting to be made to blossom like the rose. For every encounter with meaning-lessness is an opportunity to become a catalytic conductor through which new relationships are established, the forces of chaos weakened, the universe of meaning enriched, and God glorified.

If, for example, the relationship of my country to Communist China is such that it is destructive of relationships, then I may commit myself to changing the attitudes and policies which inhibit the realization of meaning and to creating new relationships which will increase the quality of experienced meaning. Such a task may be incalculably difficult, given my limited time, knowledge, and political power, and given the additional and considerable recal-citrance of the government in China. But such an activity is not meaningless just because it is so largely powerless. Such a concern and commitment becomes an actual fact within the existing world. And if it is true that it is a numerically insignificant fact, it is also true that it is precisely the kind of fact out of which, when the proper time comes, significant relationships may be born and the world of meaning extended. Meanwhile, such a concern and com-mitment functions as a witness to the kind of relationships which broaden the range of experienced meaning. As an act of witness and discipleship, it is meaningful even if ignored by those in power, overwhelmed by circumstances, and lost to future historians. For as an existing fact within the structures of reality, it is related to God, supportive of his own hope, and so meaningful for him.

The struggle, therefore, is important. In biblical history the decisive character of discipleship is uniformly interpreted in terms of this struggle to bring meaning out of meaninglessness. In the midst of a desert of personal doubt and Canaanite depravity, Abraham struggled for the promises of the Covenant; against the oppressive politics of Egypt and the recalcitrance of his own people, Moses struggled for national freedom and moral fidelity; contrary to the syncretism, selfishness, and sin of their people, the prophets struggled for justice and peace; in opposition to the self-righteous-ness of the circumcision party, Paul struggled for faithfulness to the way of love; contending with the sins of men and the power of demons, Jesus struggled for the Kingdom. The work of discipleship is consistently understood in terms of struggle, of creative and courageous contention, of fighting the good fight and finishing the race.

The significance of the struggle, however, is not in the struggle itself, but in the struggle for the maximization of meaning within history, which the New Testament describes as the reconciliation of the world, which it symbolizes in the phrase *Kingdom of God,* and which is the hope of God for *shalom.* For biblical faith, *shalom* is the final goal toward which a *meaning-ful* life moves. It is with reference to this value that all other values are understood and accredited. Plato's classic summation of values—as the good, the true, and the beautiful—takes on even richer significance when interpreted in these terms. The "true" describes our knowledge of meanings (relationships); the "beautiful" expresses our appreciation of meanings; the "good" or "just" is the establishment of conditions under which existing meanings may be appreciated and the creation of new meanings encouraged. Of course, the prophetic witness is very clear about the priority of justice over truth and beauty, because the appreciation of truth and beauty on an ever widening scale depends upon the successful implementation of justice in society. Nevertheless, justice was made for man, not man for justice, and the prophetic concern for justice, righteousness, mercy, and peace are important only because they describe the circumstances in which the optimal and universal appreciation and creation of meaning may be realized.

Man's life is fulfilled in the appreciation of existing meanings and the struggle to create new ones. The New Testament's phrase "Kingdom of God" symbolizes the maximization of such meaning within the actual world. This phrase "within the actual world" is important, because Jesus taught his disciples to commit themselves to the coming of the Kingdom within history, to work and pray for its realization "on earth." There is no discipleship apart from this struggle to deepen community and create *shalom* within history. When such a struggle succeeds it broadens the range of the meaningful world for man and for God. But such a struggle may fail. A man's power to create may be impotent before the forces of fate. Yet, even when fate has nullified our power to create, it is possible to transform the meaning of fate, making it the bearer of the meaning it appeared to destroy (pages 28-35). No struggle to creatively actualize hope and expand the range of the meaningful world is a total loss. For every such struggle to actualize new relationships "on earth" is itself a factual event within the structure of reality, an experience grounded in, and so related to and meaningful for God. In him the loss of newly established relationships is real, but also real is the struggle for their achievement.

The Question of Final Destiny

What is the meaning of life in the perspective of death? A helpful answer to this question only emerges when we are prepared to seek an answer to the further question: *What is the meaning of life and death in the perspective of God?* It is a question impossible to answer fully, difficult to answer at all. Without speculation there is no answer. But speculation need not be chaotic, dogmatic, fanciful, or arbitrary. It can and should be both grounded in experience and disciplined by logical consistency. Theology must have the courage to speculate. And theology must have the integrity to keep its specualtion disciplined.

The content of such speculation has traditionally been called the "Christian hope." In keeping with the distinction made in Chapter III, it is important to be clear on how the Christian hope is a genuine hope, and to distinguish it from mere wishing. Wishing is the arranging of symbols into patterns which are attractive, but incapable of actualization. An authentic hope must be an actual possibility. Hopes do not automatically become real. But they must be capable of becoming real.

The analysis which follows is a speculative hope—impossible to verify given present conditions, but not impossible to imagine as an aesthetic speculation consistent with our present knowledge. This proposal is a genuine hope, distinguished from a mere wish, because: (1) although it is not (yet) human experience it is grounded in human experiences; (2) although it is not (yet) what we know it is consistent with what we know; (3) although it is not (yet) what we know it is contradicted by nothing we know;

(4) although I cannot myself actualize it I can do something which partially actualizes it; (5) although it is finally dependent upon God it does not require of God anything which is incompatible with the understanding of him already outlined in previous chapters.

The meaning of man's life is realized in appreciating structures of relationship, constellations of meaning, actualizations of *shalom,* and in the creation or enhancement of structures of relationship, constellations of meaning, actualizations of *shalom.* But what is to be thought about the man who fulfills the meaning of his life only to have it ended by death? Does not the fact of death threaten —even cancel—the meaning of life?

It must first be pointed out that existence beyond death, even for eternity, does not assure the meaning of life. A life that is meaningless is not made more meaningful by extending that meaninglessness forever. Alternatively, a life that has been meaningful, even if it should not survive death, will eternally have been meaningful. The point is made beautifully by the Viennese psychotherapist, Viktor Frankl (*Man's Search for Meaning,* pp. 122, 123. Reprinted by permission of the Beacon Press, copyright © 1959, 1962 by Viktor Frankl):

The only really transitory aspects of life are the potentialities; but the moment they are actualized, they are rendered realities; they are saved and delivered into the past, wherein they are rescued and preserved from transitoriness. For, in the past nothing is irrecoverably lost but everything irrevocably stored.

Thus, the transitoriness of our existence in no way makes it meaningless. But it does constitute our responsibleness; for everything hinges upon our realizing the essentially transitory possibilities. Man constantly makes his choice concerning the mass of present potentialities; which of these will be condemned to nonbeing and which will be actualized? Which choice will be made an actuality once and forever, an immortal "footprint in [*sic*] the sands of time"? At any moment, man must decide, for better or for worse, what will be the monument of his existence.

Usually, to be sure, man considers only the stubble field of transitoriness and overlooks the full granaries of the past wherein he has salvaged once and for all his deeds and his joys and also his sufferings. Nothing can be undone, and nothing can be done away with. I should say *having been* is the surest kind of being.

. . . To express this point figuratively we might say: The pessimist resembles a man who observes with fear and sadness that his wall calendar, from which he daily tears a sheet, grows thinner with each passing day. On the other hand, the person who attacks the problems of life actively is like a man who removes each successive leaf from his calendar and files it neatly and carefully away with its predecessors, after first having jotted down a few diary notes on the back. He can reflect with pride and joy on all the richness set down in these notes, on all the life he has already lived to the full.

And now we must explore more fully what it may mean to speak of "the full granaries of the past" wherein "nothing is irrecoverably lost but everything irrevocably stored."

The oldest, most certain, and most familiar evidence for how men overcome death appears in what may be called *survival in society*. All men today are conscious of being the heirs of previous generations. The great Greek philosophers, the Hebrew prophets, the Roman lawyers, the Arab mathematicians—Luther, Shakespeare, Jefferson, Lincoln—all these have contributed constellations of meaning to the historical process which continue to survive their own limited lifetime. In some sense every society stores in the granaries of its present contributions from its past. Even preliterate societies know themselves to be benefactors of great figures from their tribal past, through legend and taboo. Writing makes these contributions more precise, and education makes them more available. In this sense we may speak with confidence of social survival. The meanings created and enjoyed by individual human lives may survive their individual death, be stored in the granaries of the socio-historical process, and available as rich sources of qualitative meaning in the present.

No one can question the truth of survival in society. What can be questioned is its value for the average man, who is not a Luther, Shakespeare, Jefferson, or Lincoln, but who is wondering about the implications of death for the meaning of his life. Many Old Testament writers seem resigned to social survival as the only "answer" to death, and ancient Hebrew men sought to "survive" through their sons and grandsons. Such survival is not to be depreciated. We all know of individuals the quality of whose lives has enriched us, and who thus live on in and through us. But by New Testament times there was a widespread recognition of the limitations of social survival.

The first of these limitations can be stated this way: while Jefferson contributed meanings to the future (for example, the Declaration of Independence) which survived him, it was not Jefferson that survived. Society may preserve my objective contributions, but it does not preserve *me*—the subjective, thinking, willing, feeling, presiding self. Without survival of the presiding self death means only the continuation of my creative contributions. It cancels both my ability to create new meanings and my ability to enjoy meaning already created. Of course, it is possible that social survival is the best we can hope for. No amount of wishing for subjective survival is going to make it so. But the New Testament spoke of "resurrection," and the early church of the "soul," with an impressive confidence—as though they had discovered something about the presiding self's possible survival. We will return to this idea shortly.

The second weakness in the theory of survival in society— for men concerned with the meaning of life—is that we do not really determine what, if anything, survives us. Usually, society must appropriate that which is going to survive, and what society chooses to find meaningful from us may be quite different from what we would choose to have survive us. I may wish, for example, to contribute to society what I believe is beautiful poetry, whereas society may appropriate only the fact that I was an accident-prone driver. Or, society may choose to appropriate nothing from me. And, if I have no family or friends, and the census bureau overlooks me, I may not survive even as a statistic. Clearly, most men cannot contribute constellations of meaning comparable to those of Luther or Lincoln. Social survival gives little hope to their lives.

The third weakness in the theory of survival in society is that it postpones but does not really solve the problem of meaning in the face of death. For what if the society dies? Surely, then, the question as to the meaning of life in the perspective of death must again be raised.

A far more satisfying (though less provable) answer to the question is what may be called the theory of *survival in God*. According to this position, although society does not preserve the full spectrum of meanings which I create—God does. The main outline of this position has already been described in previous chapters. I live and move and have my being within the life of God. My life is grounded in the divine life. I am able to appreciate other constellations of meaning (patterns of relationship between objects, events, persons, and ideas) which are also ultimately grounded in him. Correspondingly, God is able to appreciate constellations of meaning created by me. The purpose of my life consists in enjoying and glorifying God. When I fulfill the purpose of my life the life of God is enriched. The facts of my life then become aesthetic data enhancing the divine life.

This speculation is not without some parallel in human experience. At this moment I am able to appreciate memories from childhood which focus upon my dog. I recall his faithfulness and obedience, his skill as a bird dog, and his playfulness as a friend. His memory enriches my present life with a constellation of meaning which centers on him, but which also includes things (birds and fields), events (his fighting with another dog), persons (parents and friends), and ideas (mostly fantasies). I experience that constellation of meaning with a spectrum of emotions. But it is an actual contribution to my life which includes data that enables me to do what I might not otherwise be able to do (for example, approach dogs without fear).

Now, in an analogous way, we ourselves may be the center for constellations of meaning which enrich the life of God, augment the quality of his feelings, and provide data enabling him to do tomorrow what he could not do yesterday. There is nothing fanciful about this analogy. It certainly is speculation. But as such, it is a logical extension of knowledge grounded in human experience. It is in continuity with what we know, and contradicted by nothing that we know. And it is consistent with what the whole previous analysis has meant by "God."

God is the divine ground of meaning because of whom the meanings I create are not lost. But if the above analogy is to be taken seriously, then there are negative as well as positive realities for God to deal with. There were times when my dog did not obey me, and on one occasion he chased a skunk. How does human *sin* contribute to the life of God?

The answer has already been analyzed in previous chapters. The cross of Jesus is the decisive symbol for what human sin does to God. God is the eternal sin-bearer, who suffers because of the fractures in meaning and the failures to achieve meaning that follow from human unfaithfulness. What some Palestinian Jews and Roman legionnaires did to Jesus, we all do to God when we fail to be self-critical, fail to actualize *shalom,* fail to live meaningfully. God is hurt by our faithlessness as surely as he is blessed by our faithfulness.

This conclusion is not only implied in the Christian symbol of the cross, it is the logical implication of understanding the world in which "we live and move and have our being" as the body of God. This means that, *as a matter of present experience,* God knows joy and pain, the beautiful and the ugly, blessing and suffering, the meaningful and the meaningless. He is the victim of our sin and the benefactor of our faithfulness. And we experience this twofold power to affect God as the guilt and the glory of human existence.

Because of (1) human freedom and (2) our having our being in the body of God, God is not simply free to choose his present experience. That is the meaning of the cross. But he is free to choose what of the accumulating past he will remember and value. That is the meaning of *judgment.* This means that, *with reference to past experience,* God is able to appropriate what is meaningful, aesthetic, useful, and blessed for him. To be judged is to have one's life (and the events which collectively constitute

it) remembered or forgotten, accepted or rejected, appropriated
or discarded, claimed or disowned, aesthetically useful or aesthetically useless, meaningful or meaningless to God.

All that happens in the world God experiences, and all that
he experiences is available to his memory. In this sense God is
able to say, "I remember all their evil works" (Hos. 7:2). But
God is able to exclude from *living* memory these same evil works.
In this sense he is able to say, "I will remember their sin no
more" (Jer. 31:34). Like an editor working on a manuscript,
God is able (as we are able, in a limited way) to select those
memories which enrich his living present and to exclude from his
living present those sins which disrupt and distort the meaning of
the whole. In this way God exercises judgment.

The Old Testament writers tend to rejoice in God's ability
and willingness to "remember their sin no more," for they understand this to be both righteous judgment and forgiveness. They
do not rejoice in the thought of God forgetting *them*. Death
threatens life with meaninglessness precisely because the dead
may be "those whom thou dost remember no more" (Ps. 88:5).
It is one thing for God to forget the sin, but quite another for him
to forget the sinner, "Remember not the sins of my youth . . .
remember me" (Ps. 25:7). To be forgotten by God, rejected from
his living memory, is to have one's life condemned to meaninglessness. It is not death, but to be forgotten by God, which threatens
the meaning of life. Job does not fear death; he fears being forgotten. He prays, "Appoint me a set time, and remember me" (14:13).

And now, we must ask what it means to be a part of God's
living memory, what it means to be remembered by him. Mindful
that any answer to this question is a venture in hoping, I want to
suggest that to exist in the memory of God means more than to
be a closed chapter, on file, and cataloged by divine data processing
(though it also means this). I believe it may mean personal survival.

The history of thought regarding personal survival is not
particularly distinguished. In the West, the most influential theory
of personal survival was given classic expression by Plato, who
argued in favor of an "immortal soul." The chief problem with

the idea is not that an immortal soul has consistently avoided detection (though that *is* a problem), but that an immortal soul is not needed to account for any known human experience. Probably the idea did preserve the truth about the human self's capacity to preside, when men were tempted by scientific models to understand themselves as mere machines, and to understand psychic experiences as mere static or epiphenomena. But, the presiding self is a natural creation, and there is no evidence of its being *immortal.*

Nevertheless, it is *conceivable* that the presiding self survives death. And, the main problem in discussing survival is deciding what is conceivable, since we obviously have no evidence. It is conceivable because we already know *from human experience* something of the presiding self's partial freedom over its biochemical ground (as when it fights to stay awake or drinks coffee to "clear the mind"). It is at least thinkable that the presiding self can, when necessary, jettison its dead body much in the way that an infant abandons its placenta. But—since subjectivity is a companion of objectivity, from amoebas and spiders to dogs and men —it would be inconsistent with what we know to imagine the presiding self existing as a piece of floating subjectivity apart from any objective grounding in an organism. I want, therefore, to suggest that the presiding self, cut off from its body, must, if it is to survive, become grounded in the mind of God, which is in turn grounded in the objective world. This is the presiding self's "resurrection"; its "spiritual body" (1 Cor. 15:44) is its direct grounding in God.

It is possible to "get at" this argument another way. The spider evidences little capacity for memory, little ability to "hold" in his present the experiences of yesterday. The dog is much better at this. He obviously is able to "hold" impressive experiences in his memory, though apparently he cannot call them up at will, and depends upon trigger mechanisms to make memories a part of his present experience. Man is not only able to call up memories at will, but he is able to "hold" them in the present with such intensity that he ignores all that is going on about him, so that memories become for him his present experience. It is consistent with this evolutionary logic to conceive of God's memory as being able to "hold" not just vivid memories (as man can do) but something of the remembered realities themselves. To be a part of God's living memory may actually mean *to be there.* The presiding self may find its eternal home as a living cell in the mind of God. Perhaps this is what the New Testament means when it says "For you have died, and your life is hid with Christ in God" (Col. 3:3). Such a "resurrection" faith is not confidence that man possesses immortality; it is confidence that the Immortal possesses man, that not even death "will be able to separate us from the love of God" (Rom. 8:39).

If the meanings which we create pass with our death into a forgotten void, then life is indeed meaningless. Death does threaten to cancel the meaning of life. Only if our lives are meaningful for God can it be said that death is conquered, "swallowed up in victory" (1 Cor. 15:54).

To affirm that our lives are meaningful for God is to reopen the grand, metaphysical question by proposing an aesthetic answer. That answer suggests that out of the admitted ambiguities of nature and history God unites in his living memory the constellations of meaning which we create, the constellation of meaning which we are, and the larger constellations of historical meaning in which we participate into a meaningful, divine biography—a continuing story whose chapters are achieved by struggle, whose plot is *shalom,* and whose glory is to make glad the life of God.

Man lives his life within the divine life. In turn, God encompasses man—on his right hand and on his left. God is Alpha and Omega, the beginning and the end. When man looks to the future, he encounters God as the crown of hope, providing a context for human hope, filling man with the holiness of what ought to be. When man looks to the past, he encounters God as the ground of meaning, providing a context for human meaning, filling man with the holiness of that which has been. Between these poles of the future and the past, between hope and memory, lies the meaning of human life—for God.